# PARTY STYLE

*Kids' Parties from Baby to Sweet 16*

# GEMMA LYNN TOUCHSTONE

*from the hit blog www.ilovepartystyle.com*

# PARTY STYLE

*Kids' Parties from Baby to Sweet 16*

> FRONT TABLE BOOKS <
AN IMPRINT OF CEDAR FORT, INC.
SPRINGVILLE, UTAH

ISBN 13: 978-1-4621-1717-8

Published by Front Table Books, an imprint of Cedar Fort, Inc.
2373 W. 700 S., Springville, UT 84663
Distributed by Cedar Fort, Inc., www.cedarfort.com

Library of Congress Cataloging-in-Publication Data

Touchstone, Gemma.
Party style / Gemma Touchstone.
    pages cm
Includes index.
ISBN 978-1-4621-1717-8
1. Parties--Planning. 2. Entertaining--Planning.  I. Title.
GV1471.T68 2015
793.2--dc23

2015015750

Cover design by Lauren Error
Cover design © 2015 Lyle Mortimer
Edited by Justin Greer

Printed in China

10 9 8 7 6 5 4 3 2 1

Anthony & Me

My Mom

The Kids

Mom & Granmother

Dad & Nancy

Jeanette

## > DEDICATION <

This first book is dedicated to my mother, Dolly, for giving me my love of holidays and entertaining at home.

My father, Darryl, for always believing in me.

My children, whose dreams are the source my inspiration and my love.

Anthony, for grounding me and my creative brain—without you, this book would not be possible, along with too many other things to count.

Jeanette, for always being willing to shoot my style.

And to all the www.ILovePartyStyle.com fans, whose continued support provides all opportunities for the Party Style brand.

Thank You, Thank You!

XOXO

# WELCOME TO PARTY STYLE

# CONTENTS

Make a Wish
On a Starfish

## > A WISH FOR THE STYLE MAKER IN YOU <

To me, style and love go hand-in-hand. It is what we seek out in life that make us feel good, that makes us feel inspired, and that makes us feel alive and in love with our lives. There truly are so many variables to a style, and each person has the ability to create their own individual style by really focusing on what they love, what colors, textures, feelings, objects, and shapes conjure emotion. True style is developed by separating the likes from the loves, by meshing contrasting feelings, and by being able to convey a message visually.

My style shines through as I create parties, displays, and pretty settings that hopefully will make you feel something and inspire you to create amazing moments in time to share with the people most important to you. I like to think of planning and styling as an art, and a place in time is my canvas. With my art I aim to create a lasting feeling, a memory that each guest gets to take home and enjoy for years to come. Party planning is the most fun part of the experience for me. Getting to craft something special with a friend or a sister, staying up all night, rushing to get it done, trying hard to get it right, laughing at the things you missed or the things that go wrong—as they sometimes do, no matter how well you planned it out. These are the moments that you'll cherish, the fun working and the working before the fun; these are the stories that make up our lives. My wish is that we make magic together, whether it be through this book or my blog, or as you use my products to make memories in your home. I wish to inspire you to create meaningful, memorable moments with your family and friends that will last a lifetime. Embrace your true style and make your party shine with originality and personality. The fun thing about design is with the basic principles in play you can create something beautiful, stylish, and all your own.

# A PERFECT PARTY

*chapter one*

If you want to have a perfect party, then you have to have perfect planning. While there are many, many things to consider when planning your party, you will need to focus on "what the party is about" to get the planning started. Doing your best to be organized about the event details is the key to making the hosting a breeze and making your party go off without a hitch. It will make all the difference in the world for you if you sit down and plan out your vision. If you take a minute to visualize the party, who it is for, and what will make that person smile, then you can get the ball rolling on everything else. To start, write out a description on paper or on your tablet. Then, based on that description, write down your plan. This pre-planning description will save you time, save you money, and save you from stress come the day of your party. This should also be the very first thing that you put in your party-planning folder. The party-planning folder is an effective tool especially for first-time planners as you go through the process of organizing a little party for your child's birthday with all of their friends. To them, this party is a really, really big deal. Be prepared, plan well, and keep your party-planning folder up-to-date and you will not let your little one down.

## YOUR PARTY-PLANNING FOLDER

As I give suggestions to people just starting out as planners of parties both big and small, I always start off with the very same recommendation: create your party-planning folder. It is a basic tool for planning an event, be it small or large, and the folder works with children's parties or 80th birthday parties. Start with a folder like any two-pocket folder that can be found at a office supply store. If the party is going to be a larger one, then I like the Poly two-pocket folders with the three-hole punch so that I can bunch them up in a three-ringed binder. It doesn't matter if you use a Pee-Chee folder or a Top Grain Leather Padfolio Organizer Planner, as long as you have a folder dedicated to keeping track of all of your plans, budgets, orders, and receipts for your party. On our site IlovePartyStyle.com, we have a really cool party planner workbook that can be downloaded and printed with checklists and sample sheets to get you started on your party-planning folder. The basic information that you will want to keep track of in your party-planning folder is:

**1. PARTY PLANNING SHEET:** Helps you keep track of all of the important details in one place—the guest list, plans for food and drinks, the to-do list, and more.

**2. GIFT TRACKER:** This page is to log all of the gifts the star of the party receives, which will make thank-you cards a breeze!

**3. ADDRESS AND RSVP PAGE:** Keeps a record of all of the addresses for sending out invitations, and allows you to keep track of RSVP responses.

**4. GIFT PLANNER:** Allows you to plan gifts for birthdays or holidays, helping you keep the budget on track.

**5. PARTY PLANNING CHECKLIST:** To keep track of the important to-dos!

**6. PARTY BUDGET:** This worksheet will allow you to create a budget and track expenses for your event.

These five questions will get you started with the party planning. What type of party will it be? When is the date for the party? Where is the ideal location? Who will be invited? How large of a party will it be? I like to call these the "What, When, Where, Who, and How?" party considerations.

A successful party, big or small, will take some planning, and most of that planning will be built on your answers to the five questions above. The answers to those questions will create the overall scope of the event. As you move forward in the planning process, it helps to have a well-defined image of the party in mind so that you can effectively move through the checklist below.

## WHAT

What "type" of party you are planning on hosting is the most important question to answer because it will set the stage for a few of the other considerations. This is where the planning fun begins. If it is a birthday party for a preschooler, your entertainment and activities might be different from the options available for a sweet sixteen party. You can be more creative with party themes for kids in the tween range, age ten to twelve, than you could be for kindergarteners. The tweens would enjoy themes related to blockbuster movies but the pre-k to kindergarten guests would be more comfortable with simple themes like cowboys, pirates, unicorns, or princesses. Another consideration is if the plan is to have the guests participate in activities like pony rides, or if the entertainment will be spectator-based such as a movie.

## WHEN

When you will be hosting a party is important to consider as your success will be affected by major holidays, seasonal weather, prime vacation season, and the availability of venues. If you are having a party in May, you will be competing with high school proms for venues. Likewise, in June, there will be competition with weddings for space. Restaurants may be difficult to reserve for holidays like Mother's Day, Father's Day, and St. Valentine's Day. And if your party is in mid-August, the attendance will be affected, since it is the busiest time in the US for family vacations, road trips, and weekend getaways. Also consider the the time of day. How do you want your guests to feel? Is your event going to be quick with a few games and the regular traditions such as gift opening and cake cutting, maybe shoot for an early afternoon party? Do you want your guests to lounge around after the festivities? I think its best to go for a later afternoon party that can turn into a more intimate gathering as the night progresses. The *When* sets the stage for the feeling your guests will experience throughout the party.

## WHERE

Where you plan on hosting the party will have some benefits or restrictions inherent with the choice of venue. A party in your backyard or at your apartment complex's clubhouse will have size limitations that you need to consider. A party at the local equestrian center or a local park will require weather considerations. If you do plan on hosting an outdoor party, then you will also need to plan a backup location or "Rain Date." Also, if you are planning an outdoor party, then you should have your initial venue AND the backup plans set before you send out the invitations. If rain or snow will interfere with your plans, then you will need to list the "Rain Date," but if you can move on with the rain, then list "Rain or Shine" on the invitation.

## WHO

Who you plan on hosting will have an effect on the type of party that you can throw. If you are having a coed tween party, then a glamour party may not be the best idea—even if that is what the birthday girl wants. For a party aimed at younger kids, it is also important to consider whom you are hosting since many parents will expect that they get to stay at the party to support their child. This is especially true if this is the birthday party for a preschool-aged or younger child. If this is a party for young children, then you will need to plan on seating, food, and refreshments for a parent per child.

## HOW

How big of a party are you planning on having? How many guests? How much would you like to spend on the party? If you multiply the number of guests that will be at the party by how much you plan to spend per guest, then you will have an idea of how large the party is going to be. Create a budget accordingly. If you have it broken down into fixed costs like the venue and variable costs like table settings, you will have a good idea of what you need to cover for each additional guest.

# DETERMINE YOUR PARTY STYLE

*chapter two*

Planning and hosting a memorable party is an adventure in itself. As you embark on this adventure, you are creating an event that reflects your personal style while holding true to the interests and preferences of the guest of honor, the birthday boy or girl. Most birthday parties for young children are thrown by a parent or guardian. As the birthday candles start adding up on the cake, it is more likely that a friend or loved one will throw the party. Either way, the person planning the party has an attachment to the guest of honor and knows them well enough to plan quite a memorable event for the birthday boy or girl. At this point, you need to determine how much of the party is going reflect your style and how much of it is designed to please the guest of honor. For young kids it is easy, because they will focus more on the theme with their favorite color or their favorite animated movie character and will look past the font used on the party printables. Your party style may be patterned after your favorite party from your youth, or you may lean toward specifically designing and tailoring every detail of a theme to impress the moms of the kids as much as the kids. It is important to define your vision to help solidify the theme of the party.

## WHAT'S YOUR PARTY STYLE? TAKE THE QUIZ

## 1. WHICH TERMS WOULD YOUR FRIENDS USE TO DESCRIBE YOU?

A) Traditional, prim, and proper

B) Sharp, honest, and direct

C) Fun, playful, and spirited

D) Relaxed, social, and well-read

E) Bright, innovative, and forward-thinking

## 2. WHEN YOU LOOK FOR NEW CLOTHES, WHAT COLOR PALETTE DO YOU SEEK?

A) Basics, like navy, brown, gray, khaki, or white

B) Neutrals and blacks

C) A rainbow of bright colors

D) Earth tones, tan, brown, olive, rust, and charcoal

E) Black with touches of bold color

## 3. WHAT IS YOUR "DREAM-HOME" SETTING LIKE?

A) Traditional colonial. A separate library and dining room. Fresh flowers from the garden.

B) Over-sized couches. Mismatched dining chairs. Antique accents and quirky art.

C) Mansion in the Hamptons. Monogrammed pillows and towels. Blue-and-white striped wallpaper.

D) Grand staircase. His and hers dressing rooms. Works of craft galore. Furry pillows on your bed.

E) Modern, clean lines. Simple, open layout with smart controls. Outdoor living spaces.

## 4. FOR A CASUAL SATURDAY MORNING OUT WITH ANOTHER COUPLE, WHICH WOULD YOU WEAR?

A) Some comfortable, broken-in khakis, and a collared shirt

B) A sleek V-neck top and modern-fit straight-leg pant

C) A fun, casual floral dress or bright mixed prints

D) A pair of worn chinos and a PETA T-shirt with funky accessories

E) Your favorite jacket with a plain shirt with a pair of light-indigo jeans

## 5. WHICH OF THE FOLLOWING BEST DESCRIBES THE DECOR OF YOUR HOME?

**A)** Comfortable and traditional (think Ralph Lauren)

**B)** Streamlined, tonal, with clean surfaces (think Tom Ford)

**C)** Fun, kitschy, and unorthodox (think *Alice in Wonderland*)

**D)** Lots of rugs, earth tones, and floral prints (think 70s)

**E)** Minimalist, architectural, and sculptural (think modernist, futuristic)

## 6. YOUR DREAM VACATION WOULD BE

**A)** A London getaway. Quick visit to royal palace, Victorian tea time, and maybe a Polo match

**B)** Visit a small village. Tour the town with the locals. Sleep at a hostel

**C)** Yachting! Gourmet breakfast on the boat, fishing for lunch, strawberries and champagne at sunset

**D)** Off to Paris! Chauffeured limousines and an assistant to carry your shopping bags, of course

**E)** Anywhere where there are historical and architectural landmarks, art museums, and exotic foods

## 7. YOUR PREFERRED PJS ARE

**A)** A matching set with a button-down top and printed pants

**B)** Cute long johns and a loose tee

**C)** A simple nightie with a cozy robe

**D)** An old white ribbed tank that you stole from your guy and matching panties

**E)** A silk & lace set . . . preferably in red

## 8. WHAT IS YOUR GO-TO MAKEUP ROUTINE?

**A)** Pink blush on the cheeks, simple mascara, and curled lashes

**B)** A healthy tan and some lip gloss

**C)** Soft red lips, fresh skin, and winged eyeliner

**D)** Bronzed face with a smoky eye and lip gloss

**E)** Minimal and natural, just lips and mascara

## 9. YOU'RE MEETING YOUR GIRLFRIENDS FOR SUNDAY BRUNCH. YOU WOULD MOST LIKELY WEAR

**A)** Colored denim, striped sweater, diamond studs, and your Michael Kors purse

**B)** Maxi dress, your vintage denim jacket, boots, and crossover bag

**C)** Your favorite jeans, white t-shirt, brown belt, and ballet flats

**D)** Leggings, black tank, a leopard-print scarf, and your new YSL pumps

**E)** Low-rise jeans, a Silk Crepe Blouse, natural brown oxfords, and a Fold Top Tote bag

## 10. YOUR FAVORITE NAIL POLISH COLORS ARE

**A)** Neutral colors or French tips. They go with everything

**B)** No nail polish! That stuff is all chemicals

**C)** Red or dark red. Why mess with a good thing?

**D)** Wacky designs that you got on your girl's day out with your niece

**E)** Depends on what I'm wearing tonight . . .

## 11. YOUR SIGNATURE ACCESSORIES LOOK IS

A) My grandmother's pearls and my gold watch

B) However many pieces I can layer together. No such thing as too many rings

C) A bracelet my mother gave me and my gold studs

D) The watch DuJour worn hanging loosely and bangles on the other wrist

E) Long chandelier earrings and a perfectly matched clutch

## 12. WHEN YOU WALK INTO A CROWDED ROOM, WHAT WOULD YOU PREFER TO DO?

A) Blend in

B) Be in control and exude power

C) Be animated

D) Seem natural and easygoing

E) Make a statement

## IF YOU WERE MOSTLY A'S THEN YOU ARE ... *Classically Classic*

The Classic Party Host: Someone that loves clean lines, preppy colors, and classic party activities; you will tend to consider the guests and organization over the other aspects of the party.

## IF YOU WERE MOSTLY B'S THEN YOU ARE ... *Over the Top/Visionary*

The Visionary Party Host: You are someone that really likes to dig into the décor element and enjoys fresh flowers, live elements, extra details, and plush surroundings. You will tend to consider the décor and unique design over the other aspects of the party.

## IF YOU WERE MOSTLY C'S THEN YOU ARE ... *Party Stylist/DIY*

The DIY Stylist Host: Someone who loves to get crafty with the favors and spends hours looking through printable party packages to see what they can create. They might be obsessed with the Cricket Silhouette and might be planning out custom homemade invitations. You will tend to consider the favors and the sentimental elements more than the other aspects of the party.

## IF YOU WERE MOSTLY D'S THEN YOU ARE ... *Pinning Host*

The Pinning Host: Someone who has created board after board on Pinterest of every amazing party idea and theme and is just waiting to perfectly execute one of the boards full of ideas. You will tend to consider the food and activities more than the other aspects of the party.

## IF YOU WERE MOSTLY E'S THEN YOU ARE ... *Modern Host*

The Modern Host: Someone who thrives on new ideas and original designs. You love the feeling of a space and tend to consider the environment and the mood more than then the other aspects of the party.

**MAKE IT MEMORABLE** *chapter three*

### DETERMINING THE THEME OF YOUR PARTY

Trying to figure out how the party is to look is easier than trying to figure out how you want it to feel. Creating a cowboy theme for your six-year-old son is easy to do, but identifying how the mom of one of his friends feels when she walks in is a secondary part of the theme. Most birthday parties are thrown for the kids but are designed to impress the moms. The cowboy theme could have a cartoon feel, a fifties western feel, a dusty ghost town feel, or a regal and wealthy Bonanza feel, and still look like cowboys to the kids. Finding the ambiance that represents what you want the kids to see as well as what you want the parents to see is part of the big picture that we call the theme. It is important to get it set as a clear guide from the start to make it easier to keep the theme throughout the whole process.

### LOCATION, LOCATION, LOCATION!

Location, location, location, right? I know that the phrase is a bit overused and it would be cliché if it weren't for the fact that the location is key. First, it is the canvas that your party will be painted on and the backdrop of every memory about the party. Also, it is important to consider that the location you choose needs to be able to host the guests of the party. If you are planning on having 120 kids from your son's school in your backyard that barely has standing room for 60 adults, then you are going to have kids backing up into your house and your neighbor's house. Additionally, with the overcrowding, there will be little free space to see the decorations behind all of the kids standing shoulder to shoulder. So, your location needs to fit your theme as well as your party. If it doesn't fit your party, then you need to move to a bigger location or reduce the party size. Once you find a venue that fits both the theme and the crowd, you've hit a home run.

You will also have to consider logistics in getting all of the party guests to the location. The venue could be your house, a park, the beach, or a hall, but no matter where you decide to hold it, you need to make sure that the party guests can both travel to and locate the party without too much trouble. More than once, my kids have almost missed a party because I have had to drive in circles to find the exact location of a party at a park or on the beach that was hard to find based on the not-to-scale, hand-drawn map on the invite. This is less of a problem nowadays, with cell phones being so prevalent, but there are occasional issues when the party location is out of cell tower range.

Additionally, if you live in an area where the weather can change in a moment's notice, then you may need to come up with a backup location for the party if the weather will negatively affect the party. If the layout of the outdoor party could reasonably fit in the indoor backup location, then you've planned the backup location well. I recommend that you review the backup with the same layout and adapt the original party plan to make sure that all of the stations will fit and that you have additional backup decorations for the indoor location to keep the theme and to compensate for the lost view of the outdoor setting.

## FINDING INSPIRATION

Once the location is secured, you need to work on the artistic details. All great art starts from the tiniest spark of inspiration. Sometimes you have an idea for the look and feel of your party right off the top of your head, but other times you have to look for inspiration. What I have found over the years is that when it doesn't hit you all at once, your best option is to build that inspiration. When looking for an idea for a party for someone that I had known a long time, I thought that creativity would hit me like a lightning strike. But I had a twofold problem. First, I knew all of the different things that the guest of honor liked and her taste was quite varied. The second

issue was that I wanted to do something so special that I kept second-guessing myself and waffling on the design. So I started small by picking her favorite color and thinking of themes that went along with it.

Color is a strong reminder for people; a person's favorite color has a calming, comforting feel. Colors are also the second-strongest memory triggers for people, second only to scents. Starting with your guest of honor's favorite color is a strong foundation to build on. Start with a color palette page in your party-planning folder or notebook. You can use color markers, pantone cards, or paint chips; but you should have a way to show the actual color that you chose. You'll want something that you can physically compare to other colors so that you can visually see the difference as you hold the paint chip up against tablecloths, banners, or paper stock. You will also want to have this folder handy as you go around taste-testing cakes at bakeries or reviewing venues if you are not hosting at home. The brochures and pricelists from these places can be kept safe and handy in in your party-planning folder. You should keep your cell phone handy as you visit bakeries, venues, party stores, and craft stores so that you can take a quick snapshot of the items that you are interested in. With those pictures on your phone, you will be able to quickly and accurately compare colors, textures, and styles of different products without having to carry them around with you going from store-to-store. After a couple of days, your folder should start to fill out with brochures, invitation samples, fabric swatches, and concept sketches on napkins and real paper. A digital party planner is another way to go. You could list out all of your tasks, orders, and appointments and check them off as you go. You could attach cell phone pictures and store links to vendor websites all on your tablet or smartphone.

You can download a party planner from ILovePartyStyle.com for your computer today. As you find inspiration for the party, keep in mind what the guest of honor likes and what is the look and feel that you are hoping to achieve.

Discovering your inspiration is usually a "Eureka!" moment but it is also something that you can build towards by going through some simple exercises. Color matching with paint chips and real world items is a start, but it is not the only way to get your visual muscles working and your creative juices flowing. If you really want to super-charge your creative thought process then, jump on the information highway: the Internet. Many of the sites that most of you frequent now can be your starting block with a few adjustments. As you scroll through Pinterest looking at new homes or dinner recipes and dessert ideas, pin some of them to a board specifically about the party. Pin pictures of the guest of honor in his or her environment as a constant reminder to keep you focused and on the right track. If you refer back to it and compare new items before you pin them to that board, then you are training your mind to focus on what is most important. In no time, you will have a laser-sharp focus on what could possibly be added to the party board and what doesn't belong. As you build up the board, make a point of going through it every week to look for items that may no longer be in line with the party vision or theme and remove them. The next step would be to use many of the remaining pins to create a trend board for the party in Paint or Photoshop so that you can print it and bring it with you in your party-planning folder.

As you get to the point where you are ready to start a trend board, you should be ready to define what the color palette will be. It is important to be able to nail down two, three, or four colors as the focus for the party. Having the basic colors picked out makes it easier to select or reject decorations, food colors, and props without any second-guessing. The color palette should be used as a "deal breaker" when choosing items to include in your menu or your decorations. If it doesn't match or compliment the palette, it goes—no questions asked! No hemming, no hawing, since color is either a match or it is not. Yes or no, stay or go, and you will go through your decoration decision list much more quickly!

## PARTY TIMELINE CHECKLIST

*chapter four*

## INITIAL PARTY IDEAS—6 OR MORE WEEKS BEFORE

- Considering the guest of honor, choose the size and type of party that you would like to throw.
- Set a date for the party—this seems easy, considering birthdates don't change; but if the birthdate falls on a weekday, you may want to consider a Saturday just before the actual date or right after it. Also, take note of any holidays or school vacations near the date because that will affect attendance.
- Develop your inspiration trend board to keep track of color choices, textures, fonts, and patterns while you choose decorations, cake frosting colors, station components, and supplies
- Decide on a theme, if you want one, keeping in mind what the guest of honor likes—a favorite movie, superhero, toy, or activity. Years ago, party-planning experts would have placed this step further on in the process, but now it is the driving force behind much of the theme-coordinated items from the invitations to the thank-you cards and everything in between. Establish the theme as early as possible to get all of the related items coordinated and lined up.
- Decide the size of the party. The total number of people invited will determine location choices, food preparation, seating, and budget. The earlier you decide on the size of the party, the earlier you can develop the scope of the party.

## NEXT PARTY PLANNING STEPS—5 WEEKS BEFORE

- Draft a preliminary guest list.
- Design and/or order the invitations and thank-you notes if you will be mailing out printed invites.
- Address and stamp the envelopes for the invitations.
- Mail invitations to out-of-town guests so they can make travel plans.

- Review themed party printables at sites such as www.ilovepartystyle.com.
- List the printables that will need to be downloaded from the printable site. Cover everything that you'll need for the party—from food dish labels for food stations and menu cards to cupcake toppers and water bottle wrappers.
- Start pricing out the cost of the food, decorations, venue costs, entertainment, rentals, photographer, and party favors. Then, with those cost estimates, create a budget for the party. Set appointments with bakers for taste testing and review cake designs if you are purchasing a custom ordered cake.
- Based on the size of the party, start creating a scope of the party by listing out all of the desired items for the party from food to entertainment. Meet with the florist to discuss the floral decorations if you will be using flower arrangements in the party decoration.

## NEXT PARTY PLANNING STEPS—4 WEEKS BEFORE

- Finalize the guest list.
- Mail or email out the invitations to the local guests.
- Plan the menu.
- Plan the food preparation—from securing the appropriate recipes and purchasing the ingredients to making appointments for taste tests and samplings at restaurants for items that you are not going to prepare.
- Make a list of how far in advance each food dish can be made and compile a shopping list. Plan out the dishes.
- Place the respective orders with your local delicatessen, bakery, restaurant, or flower shop as needed.
- Plan out the serving and food presentation—from purchasing table linens, flatware, platter, cake plates, and candy dishes to hiring servers if desired.
- Prepare any food items that can be frozen.

## NEXT STEPS—3 WEEKS BEFORE

- Purchase any sodas, sports drinks, bottled water, packaged snacks, candies, and any items for the favor bags.
- If the party is a potluck, or if friends have offered to bring food for the party, coordinate what dishes will be made by whom to avoid overlaps.
- Line up any help you may need. Consider hiring a friend's high-school-aged son or daughter, or even

hire a professional to help with pre-party cleaning, post-party cleaning, or to bus tables and to serve drinks or appetizers. It would be better to have a helper that is not emotionally invested in the success of the party, as grandparents, cousins, aunts, or uncles may want to participate in the festivities with the guest of honor more than would a neighbor's son would.

## NEXT STEPS—2 WEEKS BEFORE

- Plan out the party food, snack, cake, and drink stations and draw up a layout. Use your layout and create an actual floor plan for you party space. You can use browser apps to help such as "Floorplanner," "Roomstyler," and "Autodesk Homestyler"; all of these apps and more can be found on Google at chrome.google.com/webstore.

- Set up a mock party based on your floor plan complete with a food station and cake station to double-check on serving and presentation items as well as your supply of dessert plates, utensils, and additional flatware. Also take note on what decorations will go where, taking pictures with your cell phone to remind you of what you had planned when you had plenty of time and were not rushed.

- Prepare printables and creating party favor bags for the guests.

- Clear out the refrigerator to make room for the new food coming in for the party and take note of condiments on hand that will be needed for the party.

- Plan out and purchase ingredients for the recipes for items that can keep for a week or more.

- Purchase the remaining non-perishable foods.

- Create a playlist of songs to play. If you are hiring a DJ or entertainment, share your wish-list playlist with them

## NEXT STEPS—1 WEEK BEFORE

- Sort the recipes out based on what should be made first and what needs to be made at the last minute.

- Prepare the dishes that can keep for a week or more.

- Plan out the number of plates, bowls, cups, and serving dishes needed to support the amount of food that you will have at the party.

- Call or email those invitees that failed to respond with an RSVP.

- Any table linens and cloth napkins should be ironed.

- Clean the house or schedule the cleaning service.

- Set the stage—start staging for the party by arranging the furniture and by removing the things that will be in the way, broken, or taken.
- Send out a thank-you email to those that have offered to make food or have volunteered to help out and restate what it was that each person had committed to as a reminder.
- Lay out decorations and count for the coverage that you desire. If you run up short, plan an additional trip to the craft store for supplies.
- Create final guest list with the head count broken down by boys and girls and adults. This will ensure that the final setup is adequate for the expected number of guests.

## NEXT STEPS—4 OR 5 DAYS BEFORE

- Purchase cheese platters if you are going to entertain parents as well as children.
- Polish the silver and clean crystal or china serving ware.
- Purchase the non-perishable foods.
- Notify the neighbors of the party that you will be entertaining children who may make a lot of noise.
- Set up a coat check station with a cleared-out closet or a rolling rack and hangers.
- Set up the clean-up station and supply it with baby wipes and hand sanitizer for the kiddies and Wine-Away (the wine stain remover), club soda, and Tide sticks for the adults.

## NEXT STEPS—2 DAYS BEFORE

- Remove frozen food items from the freezer and place them in the refrigerator to defrost overnight.
- Any cloth napkins should be folded or placed in napkin holders and boxed in preparation for the table setting.
- Based on your floor plan, sort and order the decorations for your party location from one end of the room to the other. Stack decorations for the food station in one pile, decorations for the drink station in another, the gift table decorations in a third stack, and party favor station decorations in another stack. Then go in reverse order around the room and place the decorations in a box. As you go in reverse order, the first section that you will be decorating will be on the top of the pile in the box and the last section's decorations will be at the bottom of the box. You can start at one end of the room and put up decorations and then move to the next section and then the next and before you know it the room is decorated in half the time.

## NEXT STEPS—1 DAY BEFORE

- Tables can be set up, including the table linens, centerpieces, and the place-settings for the guests including flatware, cloth napkins, and name cards if you are having assigned seating.
- Grab the decoration box that you packed the day before and go to town putting up decorations. Start at one end of the location and work down the line to the other end.
- Purchase flowers for arrangements and settings if a florist isn't arranging them. Make sure that there is room enough to refrigerate them or at least that there is good air conditioning. During the hottest months this task may be best completed at the crack of dawn on the day of the party at the local farmers market—or have the flowers delivered the day of, since flowers don't last well in the heat.
- Put up decorations. If you are in a venue, this may be outside of the venue's option and you will have to do this day of the event. If so, place your decorations as the first step in prepping day of.

## FINAL STEPS—4 OR MORE HOURS BEFORE

- Place the settings and flower arrangements on the tables and stations.
- Set up the food stations with party trays covered with cellophane to be peeled off just before the party starts.
- Set up the drink stations with drinks, cups, and straws.
- Place ice in drink tubs to chill the drinks before the party starts.
- Set up the dessert station with plates, forks and spoons, and napkins.

## FINAL STEPS—1 HOUR BEFORE

- Finish all of the perishable food preparation.
- Put ice in the appropriate food stations.
- Remove refrigerated food items and place them at their food station.
- Place hors d'oeuvres on serving trays ready to be served.
- Final walk through of the party area.

## INVITEE CONSIDERATIONS

When you ask grade-school-aged kids who they would like to have at their party, many kids say that they would like to invite their entire class, the kids that live in the neighborhood, and their little league team, along with all of the kids that they went to school with before they moved. This is rarely affordable, advisable, or even practical for most families, so you need to have a plan and share it with your child. If it is your child's first party, then you should look at it as a training party for your child. You want the party to be a success and for your child to have fun and you will be more likely to meet both goals if you start out small. A party including everyone that your child would like to have invited will likely be overwhelming for you, your child, and your guests. Be smart and plan a party that is manageable for you, and you will have a better chance at creating a party that is calm, comfortable, and enjoyable. If you are hosting the party in your house, then you already have limitations that you need to work with. Your house will only hold a certain number of children.

## PARTY SIZE CONSIDERATIONS

Over the years, a common guideline for the size of a birthday party has emerged as a standard since it was popularized by Emily Post: invite only as many children as your child's age, plus one. So if your child is turning six, you would invite seven children to the party. The idea behind this is to keep the party small when children are young so they are less likely to be overwhelmed. Then, each year your child learns to handle a larger group and their party should reflect that. Another constraint for party size would be how many people the venue can tolerate, so make sure that you double-check your party space for a realistic birthday party capacity. The last constraint for party size is the budget. You are not doing yourself any favors by skipping a party budget or not adhering to the one that you have created. In most households the budget will determine the party size, and that is common.

If you want to have a little party in the backyard or a large party in a restaurant so that you can invite all of your child's friends, that is great; but you shouldn't feel obligated to include the guests' brothers and sisters even if you have a large party. If a parent mentions that a sibling really wants to go to the party because it sounds so great, mention that you had only budget for "X" number of kids. Stand firm since you should have budgeted for your guest list and have planned around it. If the parent replies with an offer to pay for the extra sibling, you may consider accepting the extra child. But if you are set against any extra children, then by all means stick to your guns. Apologize and mention that you didn't plan for any extra kids.

You should absolutely not feel pressured to invite your child's entire class either. Most people don't have the budget or the patience to host the whole class, so it is okay for you to keep to a smaller get-together. Sometimes, the school will have a requirement to invite the whole class if your child passes out the invites at school. If that is the case with your child's school, then you will have make calls to the parents or mail the invites out via email or the postal service. If you do invite less than the whole class, then you should mention to your child that they should be considerate at school and not discuss the party in front of the students that did not get an invite. It tends to be more of an issue if your child's birthday falls during the school year rather than the summer months.

Some younger children would feel more comfortable with just the boys or just the girls for a gender-specific party, or just your child's closest friends that he or she plays with the most. If a small party is what your child wants, then that's what the party should be.

## LOCATION CONSIDERATIONS

You will need to consider whether you want the party indoors or outdoors. It would be easier to host a party for a larger group of children outdoors. If weather is a consideration, then you may prefer a party indoors at your home. Be realistic about the space inside of the home and tailor the guest list to fit the space you have available. Another option is to hold the party at another location such as a park, themed restaurant, your local rec center, a church hall, or even at a business that offers children's party packages, as a way to be able to invite more children. As you decide on the location, you need to adjust your expectations to fit it.

Be aware of the number of tables and chairs that you will be able to fit in to the location as well as the size of the play area. Along these lines, you need to take into account the size of party that fits with your personality. If you go over that size and the guest list grows outside of your comfort zone, you may want to include friends on hand that could help wrangle party kids, or else down-size the party to fit your comfort zone. If this is the first party that you have planned for your child then you may want to start small by targeting their best friends and make it a cozy, small affair. Once you get your feet wet with the first party, you will have a better understanding of the chaos that can occur as your child and their closest friends get energized by all of the birthday excitement. Once you have hosted a party for your child and their friends, you will have a better gauge to go by in planning the size, location, and length of the next party.

## CLASSROOM PARTY CONSIDERATIONS

Sometimes the kids want to be able to celebrate with the whole class even though you know that you don't have the space or the budget for that many children at your place. As a compromise that you could offer your child is to bring birthday cupcakes to school to celebrate with all of the kids. Just remember to make sure that it is allowed at your child's school. Ask your child's teacher if it is okay if your child can bring a birthday treat to their class on his or her birthday such as doughnuts, fruit cups, rice crispy treats, whoopee pies, brownies, éclairs, or cupcakes. Also, check for any food restrictions since some schools don't allow treats like brownies with nuts because some children have severe nut allergies. Check with the room mom, fellow class parents, or grandparents to see if they can help out in the classroom. Fellow parents may be able to pitch in and volunteer either during the party or by contributing supplies and food. Remember to plan for a quick classroom setup with simple crafts and games, easy-to-clean-up snacks and paper ware, and simple party decorations. This could save your budget and still make your child happy as well as add up to a double celebration for your child. It is also a very simple way to ensure that the whole class feels included in your child's birthday celebration.

## INVITATION CONSIDERATIONS

Now let's review the information that should be included on the invitations. Think of your party based on "what, when, where, and who" and make sure that the invitations cover the same information.

The "What" should be listed first on the invite telling your invited guests which birthday you are celebrating at the top of the invitation, such as "Noah is turning 6!" or "Noah's 6th Birthday Party" so it sinks in that the party is for Noah's 6th birthday. This will help the guest frame ideas for a gift, especially grandparents, aunts, and uncles that may be surprised to hear that Noah is that big already. Your fellow parents will appreciate the heads-up if you include the event theme and expected types of activities on the invite! You may also want to mention on the invite what the guests might want to bring to participate in the activities. For instance, you could tell them to bring a swimsuit and towel for a swim party or an old T-shirt of Dad's to be worn over their clothes for a painting party. Let the parents of the guests know if you will be providing a meal and include that in the invitations, as well. This will be especially useful to parents if your party is going to be hosted around mealtimes. Include a quick line that says "Lunch will be served before the birthday cake and ice cream" or "Pizza, drinks, and cake."

"When" should cover all of the time details of the party including the date, the start time, expected length, and a pick-up time if there is a hard cutoff for the party especially at busy venues. If the party is at a location other than your house, it is important to mention the pick-up time to avoid confusion about when guest's parents should return for their children. You can avoid the possibility of other parents hanging out by including the specific wording of a drop-off time and pick-up time by adding "Drop off at 10:00 am, and pick up at 1:00 pm" on the invite. If the party that you have planned for your child has a hard start time, then you need to highlight that in the invite. Many times a party includes entertainment that is scheduled by a third party and you have to let the parents know that the laser-tag game, or the play, or the movie starts at a certain time by including the word "sharp" after the start time. No matter how well you plan your perfect party, you will not be able to schedule the

*Happy Birthday*

# CAMP HANNAH

*The Great Outdoors*

2015

MAKE YOUR OWN PATH

JOIN US IN THE FOREST

*Hannah Grace*

- IS TURNING -

*Eight*

>>> RSVP: GEMMA 949. 555. 1234 <<<
CAMPHANNAH@GMAIL. COM
#CAMPHANNAH

perfect weather. So, if you're hosting an outdoor party, you will need to have a backup plan ready including an alternate location in the case of inclement weather. Depending on what activities are scheduled, such as pony rides at the park, you may not be able to move the activities indoors and your backup plan would include an alternate date. You may want to include the caveat and plan "B" information on the invite like, "In case of rain, the alternate date is the following Saturday, Jan. 22" so your guests know what to expect ahead of time.

"Where" the party is going to be held is not only the party location's address, but also the name of the venue and a description. Be as specific about the party location as possible. If the party is being given at your home, give your street address and a link to MapQuest, Yahoo Maps, or Google Maps or print it out and include it in the invite for the out-of-towners. If additional information is needed, like enter at side gate next to the garage, then add it to the invite. If the location is somewhere else besides your place, such as at a park, movie theater, restaurant, or church hall, then include the name of this location (Ford Park field #3, Capitol Cineplex, or Main Street Church Hall #B) and its street address. It would also be helpful to list the phone number of the location just in case a guest gets turned around on the way and needs to call for directions. Any descriptions that can help get your guests quickly to the right spot for the party should be included on the invite. Keep the location info handy in your party-planning folder in case anyone calls because they lost their invite.

"Who" is those that are going to have a great time at the party, like Noah and his best buddies, Mr. Butcher's 1st grade class, or Noah's t-ball team—and specify what they are going to get to do at the party.

Finally, make it easy for the guests or their parents to respond to the invite. Long gone are the days where you include a return envelope for the RSVP. If you put your contact information on the invite such as your phone number and/or email address, then they can respond quickly. Here are some of the more common RSVP formats used on children's birthday party invitations:

- RSVP by January 15th to Hannah at (###) ###-####.
- An RSVP to Hannah Stone at (###) ###-#### by 1/15/16 is appreciated.
- RSVP to Hannah at (###) ###-#### or your@email.com by January 15th.
- Please reply to Hannah Stone at (###) ###-####.
- The favor of your reply to Hannah at (###) ###-#### is appreciated.
- Kindly respond to Hannah Stone at (###) ###-#### or your@email.com.
- A response by 1/15/16 to Hannah at (###) ###-#### would be greatly appreciated.

And my personal favorite:

- Make sure to RSVP so there isn't a pizza shortage! Reply to Hannah at (###) ###-####.

There is no need to use the word "please" in the lines with "RSVP" because the acronym stands for *répondez s'il vous plaît*, which is literally "respond please" in French. It is best to give your phone number because when the parents call you can assuage any qualms that they might have about sending their precious little child to party with a bunch of other kids that they do not know. It will also give you a chance to talk to them and that in turn will drive up the yes to no ratio in favor of yesses. It is okay to ask guests to respond by a certain date because you need to know how many people are coming to confirm food, favor bags, and headcounts to the venue if hosting at an outside location. To do this, simply put "RSVP by January 15th" on the invitations.

## INVITATION TYPES

Nowadays, you don't have to practice your calligraphy for hours before sending out a nice invitation. In the digital age you can send out computer-printed invites or digital invites via email, text, or even with an automated website that saves time and paper such as www.partystylestudio.com, www.evite.com, www.punchbowl.com, www.bdare.com, www.paperlesspost.com, or using Facebook Events. There are even smart phone apps that you can use to manage your invitations like Sendtiment, Invitd, Smart Invitations, and now the website like B'Dare and Evite have an app. You can search for other apps in the app store on your smart phone. Check the rating on the app; 3.25 stars or more is usually a good sign, and read the reviews to get an idea if the app does what you need it to do. Some of these applications will send out the invite via email or text and manage the responses. Also, check out our site www.partystylestudio.com, and we will post reviews and links for apps that are new and the ones that do a good job.

## RESPONSES

Your RSVP response deadline should be about a week before the party unless a party location venue or food supplier needs more time, and then adjust your RSVP deadline to accommodate their deadline. Having the final head count gives you time to make sure that you have enough party supplies for all of the guests that are attending. If you mail out the invitations three weeks before the party, your guests will have enough time to plan to fit the party into their schedule and you will be able to get an accurate head count and shop for extra supplies if needed. Now the number of RSVPs that you should expect to get compared to the number that you sent out will depend on a few things. There are certain ratios of yesses that seem to stand over time. If you call and actually talk to the parents of the guests, you should expect a 70–80 percent yes rate. If you mail the invites out and do not personally follow up with the invitees, then the yesses will be at best half of the contact rate (around 35–45 percent). There are a few things that will skew these numbers. If you are inviting children of close friends and family members, you will receive a better response rate. If you are inviting children that your son or daughter has known for a few years, like classmates or sports teammates that have been on the same team for a few seasons, then your response rate will be a little better than average. If your child is new to the school, then the rate will be dramatically less. There will always be unavoidable no-shows so you may want to take that into consideration as you plan out food, activities, and favor bags. I prefer putting fun craft items (decorated unsharpened pencils, a little box of crayons, miniature notepads, a stamper, and stickers) in the goody bags so if people don't show at

least the birthday boy or girl could use them later and they won't spoil. The craft items can also be used in the piñata with or without candy.

## HANDLING RSVPS

How you handle the RSVPs, and more importantly, how you should handle the ones that didn't RSVP can make your party planning easier from the get-go. If you ask guests to RSVP by a specific date, most parents will call or email by that date. For everyone else, you may need to get on the phone to find out who is coming. This is a great time to get the kids involved, I suggest giving a list of the invited guests that did not RSVP to the children and have then ask the kids at school. If you're like me, you might have one child that it outgoing and can't wait to help, like my daughter; and maybe one like my son, who dreads having to quiz the kids at school as he is not one for party planning. Either way is okay—remember that just because a parent hasn't RSVP'd, doesn't mean that they won't show up on the day of the party with their child. It is important to budget and plan to ensure a fun party for all of your guests and yourself, so you really do need to have a head count for planning purposes. You will want to do your best to have enough food and party favors for every child who attends and avoid a guest going home disappointed.

So, as part of your planning, include a task to double-check on the lost RSVP's. Print out the guest list or pull out the extra copy that you have preprinted and in your party-planning folder and use this for the RSVP Checklist. Put a check mark next to the names on the list of the invited guests that have responded. Then go down the list of those that have not responded yet and give the parents a personal phone call. I like to mark the responses and leave blank the no-responses, check the yesses, and cross off the name for those that cannot make it to make it visually easy to see who is coming when I go back and update the final guest list on the computer. It can be a quick call—just make it short and simple like "Hello, this is Hannah Stone. I am calling to see if your daughter, London, will be able to join us for the birthday party this weekend?" If you are calling about a friend that your child really wants to have at the party, then feel free to mention that as well as how much fun their child

will have. As you make the calls the easiest way to tally the responses is on paper. Just copy the guest list sheet and keep it near the phone or have your tablet handy with the guest list open.

As you make the calls to get the RSVP responses from those on the guest list, you should be prepared to field a few questions about the party and the gift for the birthday boy or girl. Some parents will come straight out and ask you what gift to get your child, while others are more experienced gift shoppers that will ask questions like "What is Johnny's favorite color?", "Does Johnny like sports, and what is his favorite team?", and "What is Sally's favorite movie?" or "Is Sally still taking gymnastics?" Quiz your kid ahead of time and keep a list handy to answer the questions that will come up. Thanking them for asking is the appropriate way to respond and then give them a quick list like "Thank you for asking, that is so nice. Johnny loves the color red and his favorite baseball team is the Angels, his favorite football team is the Steelers, and Legos and Hot Wheels keep his attention for hours." Or you can respond with something closer to what toys your child likes such as "Oh, thank you for asking, Sally loves the movie *Frozen*, dress-up dolls, stuffed animals, coloring books, and board games." It is best that you be prepared for these questions because if you answer with "whatever" or "anything, I guess" or worst of all "it doesn't really matter," then you are not helping the other parent and, worse yet, it may come off as insulting as you are dismissing their interest in providing a nice gift for your child.

## PARTY HELP

If you haven't hosted a party for your child and their friends before, or if you are planning on having more kids than you're used to, then you may want some help. If you are looking for help, then you may want to ask a friend before you ask a relative, because the relative may be much more interested in seeing how much the birthday boy or girl is enjoying themselves than in helping. You may really want other parents on hand to help you supervise the children during the party, especially if it is at a venue or if you are hosting a lot of kids. Having extra help will also come in handy when you're hosting a group of small kids, like five-year-olds or younger. To ensure that you can get some parents to help out, you can put the request for one parent on the invite as an option. Make a point to confirm the request for the parent's attendance when you call to confirm their child's attendance for the party.

## ADDRESSING THE INVITES

How you address the invitation actually implies something to the recipient. Basically, each invitation should be addressed to the person being invited. If you want little Sarah to attend your daughter Sally's 9th birthday party, but not her siblings, then you address the envelope to Sarah Johnson. But it is completely normal that parents of smaller children will want to be there to support their child and to see how much fun they are having playing with the other children. With that in mind, sometimes children under the age of five will insist on bringing a date—namely, their mom or dad. It is helpful in putting the guest at ease since many children of this age are not socially experienced or even ready to socialize at a party without their parent being within eyesight. Most often, parents will linger in the background watching their child play, and most will be willing to help out in any way to make things go smoothly for all of the kids. If you allow them to help out as you serve cake and ice cream or to help clear the tables afterward, then you will have a chance to socialize with them and enjoy the party much more. If you know the whole family of the child that you are inviting or know that they have siblings the same age as your kids, you may want to invite the whole brood. If this is the case, then address the invitation to "Sarah Johnson and Family," "Sarah, Timmy, and Gerry Johnson," or "The Johnson Family." Or if you think of it as an afterthought as you are filling out the invitations, then you could add the words "Siblings Welcome" inside the invitation.

## HOSTING CONSIDERATIONS

Consider your guests when trying to find the best time for your child's birthday party as well as the length of the party. Starting at the beginning, with birthday parties for children three years of age or less, you'll have to take in to account that the kids don't have much endurance, so naptime is still a must. For the lil' kiddies, a one-hour party is about as much as they can handle in a group setting. After that point, you will be sure to have more than one child that is getting tired and cranky—and with kids at this age, in a party setting tired and cranky seems to be contagious. The best time of day to have a baby or toddler party is probably 10:00 a.m.–11:00 a.m. If you have a chance to check on the other kids' naptimes with their moms, you may be able to start it at 10:30 a.m. or 11:00 a.m., but still keep it to an hour in length. The party for the little ones should be short and sweet so that you can work around their nap time. An hour long is enough to give you time to take lots of cute pics and for the kids to have some playtime to burn off the cake. The kids that are in the four- to six-year-old range are a little more social, so you could easily bump up the party length to an hour and a half for their birthday party. By the time children are seven to nine years old, they can easily handle a two-hour party and will want interactive activities like pin the tail, musical chairs, or a piñata to smash. Tweens, the children between ten and twelve, are not little kids anymore and want to have a party that includes the kinds of activities that they see their teenage siblings doing. Karaoke is a fun alternative here for the teenager activities they aren't exactly ready for. Tweenagers can entertain themselves to for a couple of hours and don't mind the parents being around but they don't want a "cruise director" parent running things during their party. This longer party time gives the kids plenty of time for age appropriate activities, games, snacks, singing karaoke, and lots of cake and ice cream—especially for the growing boys that always seem to eat like bears storing up for the winter. As children get older and crest into the double-digit territory, the parties are more likely afternoon affairs, usually starting at 1:00 p.m. or 2:00 p.m. and may go two hours or more depending on the activities planned. As for the teenagers, they will likely want something a little more exciting like an activity-driven party that could include horseback riding, laser tag, manicures, or paint ball. After they hit middle school they will start to ask for evening parties with music and dancing or sleepovers.

## THANK-YOU NOTES

Thank-you notes are important because it is necessary to show appreciation for the guests' coming and spending time with your son or daughter whether they brought a gift or not. If they brought a gift, you should thank them

for taking the time to find a special gift your child. If you are close to the person, then you should include a little personal note. If you are not close to the person, then you can mention the gift and thank the giver for coming to the party. Ideally, the notes should be handwritten by the birthday boy or girl and sent within two weeks of the party. If the child is too young to write out the thank-you notes, then a parent can write it and the birthday boy or girl could sign it or if they are really young, the child can draw a happy face on the thank-you note. Perfect planning makes for a perfect party—planning the thank-you notes is no different. Some preparation is needed ahead of time: you should have a list of the gifts and the name of the guest that it came from. So if you were on top of things at the party and were able to keep your child's enthusiasm in check long enough to ask an adult to run a list before your child begins opening the gifts, then you should have no problem managing the thank-you cards. To make this job even simpler, print out the guest list before the party and bring it with you in your party-planning folder and as gifts are opened, jot down each gift beside the giver's name.

# PARTY DETAILS AND DECORATION SHOW YOUR STYLE

*chapter six*

## BIRTHDAY BANNER

Printable banners are also the way to go. You can find hundreds of Pennant Style banners in lots of shapes and sizes on Bannerbella.com or the ILovePartyStyle.com shop. These are amazing because they come with a complete alphabet and you can make multiple banners as part of your décor—just print the letters you need hole punch the top and string them together with ribbon, twine, or yarn. The ideas are limitless and you can really show your party style.

If you want something original, making a one-of-a-kind sign is as easy as A-B-C; well, actually, the C is real easy. First, you will need to look all over for letters in different styles. Check out old magazines, books, cards, packaging and my favorite: the junk mail. Enlarge each character to about 10 inches using a scanner or photocopier. At this size, all of the letters of the alphabet should fit on an 8.5 × 11–inch piece of printer paper. If you are computer savvy then you search the web for pictures of the letters that you would want to use. If you are really technologically inclined then you could layout the letters in a publishing program using your favorite font and print them on 8.5" x 11" printer paper. Next, cut out the letters and, using Elmer's glue or a glue stick, paste the letter to card stock for a sturdy backing. Tape letters in their correct order to ribbon, and hang.

## BALLOON BASH

Balloons scream celebration and there is nothing that gets a kid's attention more at a birthday party than balloons. You can create really great-looking party decorations with the most basic balloons. Create something extravagant with the vibrant colors of balloons covering the color spectrum. Don't forget metallic colors like silver and gold that can make a fantastic wall display. Or you can pick your favorite color in several different shades and create something simple and stated. Either way, you just need to blow up the balloons and attach to wall with double-sided tape. You can also buy a pre filled helium balloon or purchase a Balloon Time helium tank at your local Party City and fill them yourself. Balloons make a beautiful backdrop for a dessert table. Mylar letters to spell out a name add some serious style. Balloons never go out of style, and how you implement them into your party design—the ideas are limitless.

## PICTURE-PERFECT PARTY SUPPLIES

Sometimes the decorations that are just perfect for the party that you have in mind are only in your mind. It is up to you to get them out of fantasy and make them a reality so that your party has just the right look. Why buy decorated paper cups, napkins, and goodie bags when you can turn heads with your own custom versions? You can create your own party decorations from scratch or you could customize the standard boring party pieces like tablecloths or wooden forks. There are a wide variety of party printables online at sites like www.ILovePartyStyle.com and www.catchmyparty.com, as well as other sites. Wrap a band of washi tape around inexpensive plastic cups to make them more stylish. Use an old movie poster as a party decoration on the front door to get the party started. Use paint to give wooden cutlery a little spunk. Make a cake stand using an old plate and a candlestick. Make shapes on the ground outside leading up to your door by using flour, powder food coloring, and a stencil. Fill balloons with confetti before you blow them up to give them a custom colored look. Use a bag of coffee filters to make your own flower decor. Wrap straws and napkins in washi tape to give them a little unique charm all their own.

## MAKE A PIÑATA

Stuffed with candy and treats, the piñata is meant to be smashed apart, spilling its contents into the hands of the children clustered around it at parties. It is possible to make your own piñata with an old shipping box and colored tissue paper. I absolutely love piñatas, not only in the classic sense, but also as a décor element. You can create hearts and geometric shapes, and you can cover the piñata with tissue that's a perfect match for your event or a sparkly Mylar silver or gold. Hang three of them at different heights over a buffet table or just place a grouping of larger ones on the floor as an artistic expression to go with your theme. Piñatas are fun at any gathering.

## CAKE TOPPERS

Print out a printable bunting pattern from our site www.ILovePartyStyle.com and string across twine or thread on two skewers stuck into the cake. Or print a picture of your child and affix to a paper straw or skewer on the top of the cake, use a favorite toy of the child's. Or you can order a custom acrylic cake topper with your child's name from www.ten23designs.com. These toppers are amazing and provide a cool look. When it comes to topping the cake, your creativity can set the stage for an amazing, one-of-a-kind cake to remember.

## TABLE RUNNERS

Create your own table runners by using leftover wrapping paper or Recollections® Kraft Paper Rolls at Michael's Craft Stores are perfect for this. Have a blast and get creative—you can affix doilies in a pattern or paint a popsicle

stick table runner for the birthday table with popsicle sticks glued to an old length of cloth or paper. Stamp it, paint it, glitter it, or just roll it out and let the kids do the decorating as an activity.

### HANGING PAPER FLOWERS

With just a few finely placed snips and folds, and a little imagination, you can turn humble paper bags into party-perfect decorations. Or try trimming cupcake wrappers with a scalloped cut to create your own paper flower look. Paper flowers are all the rage! Pin them to the walls, hang them from the ceiling, or create an entire wall of multi-sized paper flowers all in a monochromatic style or a colorful garden. Now, paper flowers can be tricky especially when creating them 12 inches or larger. You can buy kits, take a class like the one offered by Tina Fischer Designs, or buy them premade. Creating a wall of paper flowers takes commitment but is well worth it!

### FLORAL POM-POMS, HONEYCOMB, MEDALLIONS

Dahlia and sunflower-like bursts of color hang from the ceiling, adding charm to any party. Bright tissue-paper pom-poms can be made in the size and color of your choice. Just let your imagination run wild. These look beautiful when combined with tissue honeycomb in multiple colors and shapes, or you can poof out half of a pom and create a design across a wall as a focal point for your party décor. You can find Honeycomb and medallions at Michaels Craft Stores, www.shopsweetlulu.com and our site www.ILovePartyStyle.com shop.

### HOMEMADE STREAMERS

Crepe, oh how I love thee—this is the most versatile party element. You can twist, wind, braid, and curl crepe paper. You will get a lot of bang for your buck with this affordable party material. Stripe a doorway with a few different colors. Cut into confetti pieces, fringe cut sheets and twist into a backdrop for a serving table, or add to straws and wrap gifts. Use 3M painter's tape to adhere the fringed curtain to the wall. The ideas are endless. I always have a stock of every color.

### SHIMMERING STREAMERS

Leftover wrapping paper gets a fresh start when used to make decorations for a party. Just use metallic sheets available at Michaels Craft Stores to make streamers of shimmering circles that descend from above.

### FLAG STREAMERS

Measure out and draw the template to size on to piece of plain paper, then cut it out. Trace it onto a scrapbook or other decorative paper, and then cut out the flags. Next, cut twine as long as you want the streamers to be. Apply Elmer's glue or a glue stick to top of a flag, on back. Wrap the glued edge around twine, folding resulting flaps forward, and securing them on the flag's front. Repeat with each of the remaining flags.

### KEEP IT GREEN

If you're hosting a birthday party and want to make it a "green" party that's just as good for the environment as it is for the kids, then forget the plastic and go paper—paper plates, paper tablecloth, and all-paper decorations! My favorite "green" party craft is to make a tiered cupcake stand by using paper cups as the base and a paper plate as the cupcake plate. Recycle when done!

### FESTIVE GARLAND

Letter-perfect party decor is easy to create with a garland made by using a clip-art alphabet. Create a personal birthday greeting in tones that match the rest of the party and hang above a serving table done up in similar shades and tones as the table decorations. Sew a cute garland with tissue paper flowers. Turn your leftover cupcake liners into a colorful garland. A homemade banner can pack a big decorative punch. Put in a little love and care and these homemade designs can be reused year after year.

### WALL DECORATIONS

Use a projector to shine a picture as a template onto the cardboard and then trace and cut out the shape that you wanted. The cutout will make a giant sign that you can then hang over the treat table.

### TABLESCAPES

Decorating the kids table is a fun way to making your little guest feel special. Using different colors and textures on the table can make it exciting. Add special treats to make each individual guest feel like they were thought of. Tablescapes for kids are fun and really make them feel all grown up.

### PRINTABLES

What is a party printable?

Simply stated, it's a downloadable PDF of a graphic created for you to cut out and use. DIY party printables are all the rage. To work with printables, you will need a couple fun tools in your party crafting kit. I suggest the following:

- Party punches—I use a scallop, a 2-inch circle, and a flag punch all the time by EK Success
- Sharp scissors
- 2 types of hole punches, Friskers brand
- A circled cutter
- Fringe scissors by Martha Stewart, and mini scissors also by Martha Stewart, available at Michaels Craft Stores

It helps if you have a cutting mat. You can order custom printables on our website or from many amazing, talented graphic designers found on Etsy. I recommend using card stock and an Epson Laser Jet printer for printing. The following is a list of must-have party printables for any children's party to create that chic personalized look.

> *Invitations*

Today you can design and print party invitations at home with die-cut and printed cards that are ready to run through your ink jet printer. Or you can find professionally designed invitations that you can customize and print at home. Some styles you will find will be paired with matching lined envelopes or you can create your own signature envelope with party crafting papers.

Whether you buy ready-to-print or specialty designed, printed invitations are the way to go for that polished and planned look and feel for your event.

> *Signs*

Party signs have to be my absolute favorite way to dress up a party, and they are also the most cost-effective way to make a big impression, hands down! The best part is that they are the easiest way to decorate. Signs are usually offered in 5 × 7–inch and 8 × 10–inch sizes so framing is an absolute breeze. They're so cute and easy!

## WHAT YOU NEED

- A strip of paper (custom designed or just printed scrapbooking paper) 1¾ inch tall and 8½ inches wide.
- Paper cutter, but you can use scissors. I just like my cuts straight.
- 2-inches-wide clear heavy duty packing tape
- Water bottles—my favorite to use based on style are the Target store brand by Archer Farms or the Aquafina alkalized water.

## INSTRUCTIONS:

For ordered labels, the labels sometimes come as stickers. If they are stickers, you just evenly stick them around the label portion of the water bottle. You can also use glue dots for a simple label option for a label that will fight bottle condensation. I like to make mine as shown here.

1. Cut out your strip of paper to create the label and then lay your label out on the table.

2. Cut a piece of packing tape slightly larger than the label or piece of scrap paper leaving about ½ inch on each side of the paper.

3. There will be a piece of tape coming over the sides of the paper. Fold it over and smooth it out evenly.

4. Line the label up as straight as possible along the side of the bottle, fold the tape into the bottle and same with the other side, they should line up perfectly.

### > Water Bottle Labels

Single serving water bottles have become a party standard in today's party throwing society. I love having them at family gathers and kids' parties. Creating water bottle labels has never been easier than it is today. There are two ways to customize these convenient drinks: you can order a customized label designed by a graphic designer or a talented Etsy seller, or you can create semi-waterproof labels with your favorite scrapbook papers. These decorative wraps can also be used as napkin rings.

### > 2-inch Party Rounds

Who doesn't love Party Circles? These cute 2-inch circles can serve many decorative purposes and be a stylist's best friend. Usually, they are sold in one sheet of twelve styles with four designs. You will want to have an EK Success 2-inch punch to create the perfect round. I love to use these party rounds as thank you tags, garlands, centerpiece décor, and cake toppers, but you will usually see them as cupcake toppers.

### > Party Flag

Party Flags are the best way to add sweet details to drink stirrers, paper straws, toothpicks, cake buntings and more! I love party flags because of their versatility. You can print them on paper and use double-sided tape to adhere the sides together and around whatever your embellishing, or you can print the little flags on adhesive label stock that you can peel and stick. Flags are offered in various sizes and styles. For the true look of a flag, you can create inverted triangle on the tip to leave a blunt cut. Your flags are as creative as you are. With a pair of little scissors you can create all kinds of looks and feels.

### > Banners

Every party needs at least one banner. Sometimes a large "Happy Birthday" is all that's needed. Maybe you want to point out stations with a homemade bunting for Gifts, Sweets, Drinks, Favors, Games, etc. I love Bannerbella Printable Banners at www.bannerbella.com because she sells each set for only $10.00 and it includes the complete uppercase and lowercase alphabet so you can spell whatever you want. She also sells them pre-cut, hole-punched, and ready to party! All you have to do is add your favorite ribbon, twine, or string.

### > Tent Cards

These are ideal for labeling food, drinks, place settings, and more! You can get creative with the uses for tent cards, and even use them for games or name tags. When you purchase printables from the Party Style Studio, we always include popular buffet items and blank cards. The cards usually feature a stylish border with minimal graphics and are intended for use with handwritten text.

### > Thank-You Favor Tags

Favor tags are a fun way to personalize and dress up take-home goodies and treats for you guests. You will find a variety of favor tags for every kind of event and party. Simply cut and use these tags to create an awfully sweet gift to send off with your guests. You can apply and use them in a variety of ways to fit your look and theme.

### > Printed Papers That Match Your Printables

Patterned paper a great party crafting element. My favorite thing to do with printed paper is use it as a tray liner or backing for printables. With patterned paper you can create water bottle labels, make treat bags or candy cones, line vases, or even create paper flowers. It is truly limitless what you can do with printed paper.

## LET THE FUN BEGIN

### > Party Games

The intention of a party game is to keep the kids occupied. If the games are held outdoors, then you can add physical activity to the list of benefits. There will be kids that have stage fright and don't want to participate, and there are those kids that just don't take losing too well. If you find that this happens at your party, then you can adjust the choice of games to team games to get the kids to work together and to interact with each other. You also should plan some noncompetitive activities like arts and crafts. I prefer to combine the games and the crafts in games, like the "Dart Paper Airplane Flyer" game. Games like this give the kids a chance to create an airplane and color it, giving it that customized aspect, and then they compete with their respective airplanes.

### > Planning Party Games

Party games have been a long-standing tradition at children's birthday parties and you should definitely plan to have the kids participate in party games at the party.

When planning party activities, you should always have two or three more games ready than you think you will need. Having these extra games cued up could save you if the children finish a game more quickly than you'd expect. For the big kids, plan 4–6 activities with a nice mix of crafts and games over the one-and-a-half-hour-long party. For the teenager party, you should plan 5–7 activities with a mix of more games than crafts to cover the two-hour to two-and-a-half-hour-long party. As for a toddler party, it is perfectly acceptable to let the kids play freely most of the time, and if you do have planned activities one or two should be all that you will need.

Some parents actually worry that if the games that are competitive and result in winners and losers, it will negatively affect some of the kids at the party and bring down their enthusiasm. For younger children who may not have a grasp on competition and have not yet learned to be a good winner or loser, I wouldn't focus on games that you win as much as activities to participate in. Most feel that competitive party games still have their place at a kid's birthday party. The key, even with the older kids, is focus on the participation encouraging all to play, and to make the prizes fairly small, so the other children won't get jealous. You may want to consider giving out small packets of candy or stickers as prizes for the winners. Be sure to include noncompetitive activities in your party too, such as arts and crafts.

Don't act like a drill sergeant or even a cruise director. Let the children move through the activities at their own pace. Unless it runs over into mealtime or scheduled entertainment, don't push the children to finish up a game that they are really enjoying. If you have planned a game that the kids really love, they may want to play it again over and over. Never stress about getting the kids to play every game that you planned. Just let the kids drive the pace of the party and it will be a success.

Below is a starter list of games that you can hold at birthday parties. It is a starter list and something that you can build on. There are more games listed on our site www.ILovePartyStyle.com, and many other sites on the Internet have other examples. If you do a little research, you could easily find a few more games that are in in line with the theme of your party or ones that will fit the group of kids that you have attending your party.

## BACK-TO-BACK BALLOON POPPERS

Back-to-back balloon poppers is a fun birthday party game to keep kids active and laughing. This engaging kid's activity can be played indoors and outdoors and is enjoyed by children of all ages. Get popping those balloons now!

NUMBER OF PLAYERS: 4 or more in even pairs

WHAT YOU NEED: balloons

HOW TO PLAY:

Divide children into pairs.

Have the children line up back-to-back holding a balloon in between their backs.

On your command, have the children attempt to squeeze together and pop their balloon.

The pair that pops their balloon first is the winner. If you want to keep this game competitive for the teenagers, make the pair start off by picking up the balloon off of the floor and move it up in between their backs without using their hands.

If you want to have a good laugh without having a specific winner, keep the game going until all pairs have popped their balloon. There will be pairs that don't move well together and will struggle to squish the balloon hard enough to pop it. Their struggles are often good for a giggle or two.

# NAME SIX

Get your kids' minds active with Name Six, a fun game for birthday parties and family gatherings. Have fun as you keep them learning and competing to show how good their knowledge is!

**NUMBER OF PLAYERS: 10+**

**WHAT YOU NEED: Small ball**

**HOW TO PLAY:**

Choose one adult to be the leader. That leader stands aside as the other players form a circle.

Start passing the ball from player to player.

Standing outside the circle, the leader calls out one letter of the alphabet.

Whoever is holding the ball when the letter is called out has to name 6 things that begin with that letter before the ball comes around to him again.

For example, if the leader calls out "B" the player can call out, "Ball, building, bar, bug, bump, banana."

If the player fails to call out six words before the ball is passed back to them, the ball continues to be passed around the circle and the leader calls out a new letter.

Once each player has had a turn, the players who couldn't call out six words in time are out of the game.

The winner is the last player remaining who can call out six words before they get the ball again.

## SCREAMIN' BALLOONS

This one really isn't a head-to-head type of balloon game, but it is fun and has a "wow, that's so cool" factor.

NUMBER OF PLAYERS: 1+

WHAT YOU'LL NEED: A balloon for each kid, a small hex nut for each balloon (Make sure that there aren't any sharp, jagged edges on the nuts.)

HOW TO PLAY:

Drop a single small hex nut into each balloon and then blow up the balloon and knot it.

You can demonstrate the goal by gathering the kids around and asking them if they've ever heard a balloon scream. Demonstrate the "Screamin' Balloon" by holding the balloon in both hands and moving it rapidly in a circular motion. As you start to move it faster and faster the hex nut rubs against the inside of the balloon and squeaks. As the spinning gets faster, those squeaks come faster until it is just one long screamin' sound. At that point the kids will be smiling. Ask them if they can hear the balloon scream?

The goal is to have the kids try one at a time and see who can keep the balloon screamin' the longest. The rest of the kids can count it out. Older kids will be able to get the hang of this after a few minutes and make the balloon scream for a while so this game is best for the youngsters to tweens.

## BALLOON DRIBBLE

Balloon dribble is a fun activity that will excite your small children with the wonder of balloons. If you need to keep your kids busy for hours on a rainy day this is a great indoor boredom buster.

NUMBER OF PLAYERS: 1+

WHAT YOU'LL NEED: Balloons, a willing adult to blow them up (or a pump)

HOW TO PLAY:

Blow up a few balloons for each child and encourage them to throw them up in the air and keep them afloat. They will love the ease with which they can maneuver these weightless objects.

As they gain confidence (or for older children), tie a rope across two points and have them try to hit the balloon up and over. For the tweens and teenagers, they have to keep the balloons up while they use just their feet. The can use their body and dribble the balloon the same way soccer players dribble the soccer ball.

Count each hit up into the air. Their turn is over when the balloon hits the ground, another player, or any hard object around like the wall or a chair.

# DUFFER'S SPOON RACE

Get into the racing spirit with this fabulously fun party game. The kids will love the classic egg and spoon race with a golfer's twist. The duffer is the beginner golfer and in this game you must learn to balance their golf balls on a spoon and coordinate the hand-off to their partner to win!

**NUMBER OF PLAYERS:** 4+

**WHAT YOU'LL NEED:** teaspoons, golf balls

**HOW TO PLAY:**

A race of balance and coordination, the golf ball and spoon race is a classic game that will have kids giggling right up to the finish line!

Arrange all of the children at a start line with a golf ball and a teaspoon each.

When you are ready to start the race, ask them to place the golf ball onto their spoon and then place their other arm behind their back.

When you say go, the children will race—as fast as they can without the golf ball rolling off the spoon—to the finish line.

If the golf ball falls, the child starts again!

Whoever crosses the finish line first with their golf ball still balanced on their spoon and an arm behind their back wins.

# BIRTHDAY PRESENT MEMORY GAME

Tease and entertain your guests and kids with this fun Birthday Present Memory Game that will have them wracking their memory for clues. Super easy to play and no mess to clean up, you can't go wrong with this old party favorite!

NUMBER OF PLAYERS: 6+

WHAT YOU'LL NEED: paper, pens, a box, 15 small recognizable items (toys, household items, ornaments etc.)

HOW TO PLAY:

Place all the items in a box. Give the kids and guests a few minutes to look at the items in the box.

Away from their sight, take one or more items out of the box.

Return the box to the viewing table and ask the players to guess what items are missing.

Players have to write down as many items that they can remember from the box before you say "Stop."

The player with the most correct answers wins.

## MOON-SHOT BALLOON

Moon-shot Balloon is a fun birthday party game to keep kids active and entertained as they practice their "moon shot" and hope that they hit the target with their balloons. The kids get to launch colorful balloons and you get to watch the wonder and joy in the faces of your children as they play.

NUMBER OF PLAYERS: 2+

WHAT YOU'LL NEED: One balloon per player (not inflated), pens for decorating tape or string that can be shaped into a circle for the moon landing target

HOW TO PLAY:

Each child gets a balloon that they decorate with the pens to look like a UFO, space ship, or lunar lander. All children are to inflate their balloon. Some children may need help in doing this.

On your command, instruct the children to let go of their balloon in the direction of the target.

Keep score so as to determine a winner.

Allocate 5 points for the balloon that lands closest to the moon landing target and 15 points for a direct hit on the target.

This can be a fun game played in teams.

## SWEET WATER RELAY

You don't have to have a sweet tooth to enjoy the sweet water relay. This is an old-time favorite birthday party game and kid's activity. Just add kids, a cup of water, and a serving tray or charger together and the result is a fantastically fun activity for all.

NUMBER OF PLAYERS: 6+

WHAT YOU'LL NEED: 2 trays, 2 or more cups of water

HOW TO PLAY:

Divide the children into two teams and have them form lines.

Give the first child in each line a tray and a cup of water.

When you say "go," the first player in each line lifts the tray with the cup on it waiter style and speed walks to the other end of the field and back and then hands off the tray to the second person in line. If they spill the cup of water, then they have to return back to the starting line and do it over again.

The second player does the same and so on, down the line.

The team that finishes first, wins.

For the older kids there will be more cups of water at the other end of the field and they must add one more cup to the tray before returning to the next person in line.

# THE DART PAPER AIRPLANE FLYER

Making paper airplanes is a simple paper activity for kids that will lead to fun outdoor games as they fly their paper airplanes. This simple dart paper airplane design is a truly speedy flyer.

NUMBER OF PLAYERS: 1+

WHAT YOU'LL NEED: 1 (8.5 × 11–inch) sheet of paper per child

HOW TO PLAY:

Have each child make a dart paper airplane.

Start by folding the sheet in half lengthways. Open it out.

Fold the top-left corner down to the center crease (the classic paper plane fold).

Fold the top right-hand corner down to the center.

Take the left side and fold it to the center crease to make steeper diagonal angle.

Do the same on the right.

Fold the left-hand side to the center again, for an even steeper diagonal.

Do the same on the right.

Now fold each side in to the center again, for the final time.

Flip it over (so that the blank side is facing up) and fold it in half along its length.

Now pop out the wings, pinch the fuselage and give it a whirl!

You can throw the dart fast and hard, but make sure you give it lots of air, as it has minimal wing area to keep it up.

If you want to keep the children busy for just a bit longer you can offer them crayons, pencils, or markers to draw windows, doors, and jet engines on their planes.

After all of the planes have been customized to each guests liking then you can line them at the throwing spot.

Each child throws their plane as smoothly as possible to have the longest fight possible.

The child with the longest flight wins.

# BALLOON POPPING RELAY

What could be better than a balloon game where the kids get to run around and pop balloons!

NUMBER OF PLAYERS: 2+

WHAT YOU'LL NEED: Balloons (inflated), notepaper, marker, bag, box, and a basket or other type of container to hold the numbers from the balloon

HOW TO PLAY:

Write numbers from 1–25 on playing-card-sized pieces of paper, put one piece of paper with a number on it inside each balloon and blow it up. If filling balloons with helium, then strings or ribbons will be needed to tie the balloons down.

Divide the kids into two teams and have the kids form two lines about 6 feet apart.

Each team has a basket or a box to collect the numbered papers in.

Place the filled balloons at the other end of the playing field from the two teams.

On the word "Go!", the first two kids from each team must race to the balloon area, take one and pop it as quickly as they can—they can sit on it, step on it, or pop it by any other means. Once they pop the balloon, they grab the number that was in it and race back to tag the next team member in their line by dropping the numbered paper in the box or basket.

The game continues like this until every kid has had a turn. The team that finishes first, the one that has every player pop a balloon is the winner, or is it. Have an adult add up all of the numbers on the pieces of paper for each team and that is the team's score. The team with the greatest score wins.

# MEMORY CAPTURE

Get your party moving with a great game of memory. This party game is a great kid's activity for all ages and for any grown-ups who want to try and keep up too! It is played out on a large scale and the kids need to be alert to score.

NUMBER OF PLAYERS: 6+

WHAT YOU'LL NEED: 20 paper plates, 20 index cards

HOW TO PLAY:

Start by creating ten pairs of matching cards. You can put a variety of things on the cards like numbers, animals, or the kids' names—just make sure that you have two of each. Now place the cards face up randomly on the floor or grass in five rows of four cards each. Do this out of sight of the kids, and then cover each card with an upside-down paper plate. Next, divide the children into two teams. Assign Team 1 to the left side and Team 2 to the right side. Now one person at a time goes up and lifts a plate to see the card and then picks a second plate to reveal that card. If there is a match, then the child takes both cards and places the plates back in there original spot upside down. Then a member from the other team takes a turn. Keep alternating until all of the cards are collected. The team that ended up capturing the most index card pairs wins!

# WILD WIND WELAY

This is a great party game for children. They will need to use their concentration skills to get the balloon to the end of the race.

NUMBER OF PLAYERS: 6+

WHAT YOU'LL NEED: A packet of balloons, a packet of straws

HOW TO PLAY:

Mark a starting and finishing line about three yards apart.

Position the children along the starting line in two equal lines and give each a round balloon and a straw.

The children have to race on their hands and knees, blowing their balloon with the straw. They blow to the other end of the field, then pick their balloon up and race back. As soon as they get back to their team, the next person goes.

The first team to have every child reach the finishing line wins.

## PERFECT PARTY TIPS AND HELPFUL HINTS

*chapter seven*

### A QUICK RECAP: PREPARE. ANTICIPATE. BE FLEXIBLE.

> The party starts at the door! Decorate your front door with a simple wreath, a poster, a beautiful floral decoration, or a jumbo themed party cutout that lets the guest know the party is here!

> Keep the birthday party guest list to a reasonable number. The rule of thumb is one guest for each year of your child's age, plus one.

> Check with the school on their policy for distributing invitations.

> Plan ahead for an unexpected guest or two or three or, as in my family, half a dozen.

> Work with what you've got!

> If you shop around, renting can be a surprisingly cheap way to go for party supplies. Indoor/outdoor folding chairs start as low as $2 a piece. Many party rental places even rent shabby chic furniture pieces, rugs, and stools for indoors as well as farm benches, coolers, speakers, tableware, and a bigger grill for outdoors. The party rental place will even drop off and pick up, leaving you to focusing on the food, the guests, and on having a good time.

> Carve out a dedicated space for the party food station. It seems that guests blindly follow the food and drinks and ultimately, that is where everyone gathers. It also explains why there always seems to be a crowd in the kitchen.

> If you are going to include flowers in your decorations, remember to plan enough time for them to bloom for the party. A couple of days should be fine for most blossoms.

> For a party of 25, you should have a supply of about 240 napkins. When food is involved while visiting someone else's house, the guests feel that they need to take more napkins than they actually need because spilling food or ketchup on the cheek is more embarrassing than taking extra napkins. So the

extra napkins never hurt, and you could always use the extras with your own kids.

> Never underestimate the power of good lighting.

> Decorating a children's party in a pinch is a cinch. In fact, you really only need to start with one big party decoration and that's the piñata. If it is a last-minute party and you are short on time, then buy a big piñata that fits the mood of the fiesta and then decorate your place to fit in with the piñata's theme. Pick up some color-coordinated balloons, favors, and plate ware, and you have the start of a kid's party. Piñatas are colorful and create excitement for the kids with the mystery of what could be inside! It's a fun, interactive, large centerpiece decoration for kids' parties! Hand out the broomstick before the kids are too tired and let them have at it.

> Make sure your party space layout has been thought-out. You want to the make guests comfortable. Do you have enough places for the guests to sit? Do you have room for the teens to dance? And are the crudité platters easily accessible from every angle?

> Try to have plenty of adult help on hand.

> Plan and prepare for plenty of activities.

> You do not need to spend a fortune on party favors. Simple and thoughtful always works.

> Offering tea or coffee will entice three-fourths of guests will accept the invite, almost double the average acceptance rate. It seems a little like a throwback to the "Happy Days" era, but it still is a great way to complete an evening of socializing by sharing a cup of hot tea or coffee. If your party is later in the day, I'd suggest having decaf coffee on hand too. You can prepare it ahead of time and just put it back on the heat for a few minutes before serving..

> Make sure that you have enough seats for the expected number of guests. If you are having an outdoor party and you have six patio chairs and two dozen guests, put towels on the lawn or on short garden border walls to make bench seats. Do the same evaluation with your indoor furniture if you are having an indoor party. If you come up short, press dining chairs into service, include your barstools in the mix as well as your ottomans & poufs. If you're keeping things casual, you can spread out some pretty quilts on the ground with throw pillows and let people gather picnic-style.

> Prep as much of your food as possible in advance.

> A birthday party that you are hosting is not the time to try and bang out a cheese soufflé or anything else that you've never made before!

> Worst case food scenario: order pizza and the kids will still think that you planned everything out just right.

> You can pick up some dishes from your favorite takeout or even have a potluck to fill out your food station. You don't have to make everything yourself.

> A platter of finger food late in the afternoon can carry your guests until dinnertime. A crudité platter is your "ace up your sleeve," whether it is a beautiful modern platter or an old-school platter with celery sticks, broccoli florets, and carrot sticks with a ranch dip or buttermilk dressing. This is inexpensive, quick, convenient, and is a pleasing and familiar dish that gets gobbled up every time.

> Remember that you are a home cook, not a professional chef who cooks for hundreds every day.

> Reward yourself by making enough food that you have leftovers for the guests and yourself. That way, come the next day you can relax, enjoy the leftovers, and relive the party with no hard work involved.

> Plan on providing two to three drink cups per person when serving food at a party. People often grab a drink, put it down as they are talking, and then go take a new one rather than risk grabbing someone else's drink.

> Check with the guests on any food allergies. Have you ever seen an EpiPen pulled out at a children's birthday party? It's not a pretty sight. Please avoid this at all costs.

> Don't make things too complicated!

> Introduce guests to each other when they arrive.

> For teen parties, the perfect playlist is important!

> You will want to have some board games available in case there is a lull in the party, but don't overdo it. Playing board games can really cut into a guest's cheese-platter tasting time. Never underestimate the power of the cheese platter!

> Family get-togethers often go on after the party has ended. Many times the relatives will hang out even after the party has officially ended, so plan to entertain the kids for a little longer. While the grown-ups can kick back, munching on popcorn and nuts as they reminisce about the holidays or the family vacations of their childhood, you should have some diversions for the kids: have plenty of blowing bubbles on hand, a couple of Frisbees, and uninflated beach balls that they kids have to blow up to play with. You could also get a few inexpensive disposable cameras and let kids serve as official event photographers.

> Please, for the love of all that is good and holy, make sure you have enough ice on hand. This is especially important for outdoor parties even in mild weather. So . . . collect it, make it, buy it, do whatever you have to do to get it; your party can never have enough ice.

> Accept help when it is offered!

> For patio parties that go on into the evening, don't forget to check your lighting. When you roam around your yard in the evening, you know what is there, but your guests may not be that familiar, so light their way. Hang strings of lights on the patio cover, the deck, the fence, and even from tree branches in your yard. You can also add some rope lights on stair banisters or hurricane lanterns and even a trail of tea-lights. I prefer Edison Bulb light strings or globe string lights, as the elegant round bulbs and incandescent wires give off a nice, warm glow.

> A good tip for an outdoor party is to plug in some fans to cool your guests and keep away pests. Mosquitoes are not strong flyers, so even when a fan that is set to low, it can create enough airflow to discourage mosquitoes. This works great in a small area like a patio, a deck, or the area nearest to the open patio doors. Just set up two or three box fans around your party area to dissuade the pests. It is also a good idea to put an oscillating fan near your food table to blow off the mosquitoes and any flies that may want a taste of your Aunt Edna's potato salad.

> Prepare your guest of honor to greet their young guests. Teach them to say "thank you" for gifts and "good-bye" to everyone.

> It's a party! Have fun! Remember not to get too bogged down with hosting duties.

# PARTY THEME IDEAS (FOR BOYS)

- Mickey Mouse
- Pirates
- Toy Soldiers
- Legos/Minifigures
- Hot Wheels
- American Patriot/Red, White, and Blue
- Star Wars
- Farmer/John Deere
- Cowboys
- Dinosaurs
- Coca-Cola/Soda Fountain Shop
- Airplanes
- Baseball/Football/ Basketball/Soccer
- Cars/Planes (Disney Movies)
- Aliens/UFOs
- Astronaut/Space Travel/ Rockets
- Camping/Hiking/ Outdoors/Lumberjack
- Charlie Brown/Snoopy/

- Peanuts
- Mickey & Friends (Donald, Goofy, Pluto, Minnie, Daisy, Oswald)
- Disney World
- Hot Rods/Cars
- Marvel Universe: Avengers/ Thor/Captain America/ Hulk/Iron Man/Ant Man/ Spider-Man/Guardians of the Galaxy/X-Men/ Fantastic Four
- Superheroes: The Incredibles/Batman/ Superman
- Circus/Carnival
- Bicycle
- Trains
- Video Games: Halo/ Mario/Sonic/Club Penguin/Minecraft
- Beach/Surf/Nautical/Sailor
- Monsters Inc./Monsters
- Hollywood
- Big Hero 6

- Indiana Jones
- Luau/Hawaiian
- Magician
- Jungle/Monkeys/Lions/ Safari
- Comic Books
- Computers/Technology/ Nerd
- Nerf
- Tron
- Transformers
- Dragons/How to Train Your Dragon
- Camouflage
- Willy Wonka
- Knights/Kings/Castles
- Wreck-It Ralph
- Skateboards
- Scooby Doo
- Rock & Roll
- Policeman/Fireman/ Doctor
- Play-Doh

# PARTY THEME IDEAS (FOR GIRLS)

- Princess
- Minnie Mouse
- Pink
- Frozen (Disney)
- Rainbow
- Tea Party/Alice in Wonderland Mad Tea Party/Mary Poppins
- Barbie
- Country Fair/Farm Animals—Pigs, Cows, Horses, & Sheep
- Winnie the Pooh
- Artist/Painter
- Cinderella
- Ponies/Unicorns
- Teddy Bears
- Wonder Woman
- Pets: Dogs/Puppies/Kitties/Bunnies
- Toy Story
- Lilo & Stitch/Luau/

- Hawaiian
- Cowgirl/Jessie (Toy Story)
- Carousel
- Tie Dye/Neon/Glow in the Dark
- Ladybugs/Honey Bees/Butterflies
- Candyland/Candy/Sweet/Dessert
- Fairies/Tinker Bell
- The Little Mermaid
- Penguins
- Zoo
- Angels
- Pastels/Confetti
- Pandas
- Strawberries/Fruity/Cherries
- Wizard of Oz
- Pac-Man/Ms. Pac-Man
- Wall-E & Eve
- Garden/Flowers

- Glam/Diva/Movie Star
- Hunger Games/Brave (Disney)/Female Archer
- Balloons/Up
- Muppets
- Harry Potter/Witches/Wizards
- Vintage/Retro
- Diamonds/Pearls/Gold
- Pajamas
- Whales
- Picnics
- Elephants
- Pinocchio
- Once Upon a Time/Fairy Tales
- Kids' Shows: Dora/Clifford the Big Red Dog/Curious George
- Ballerina
- Crayons
- Dolls/Antique Dolls

# HOW TO Stage a Birthday Photo

## USING BALLOONS

| NO | YES |
|----|-----|

*Be sure to use a **variety of colors and shapes** for your balloon arrangements to spice things up.*

## USING A BACKDROP

| NO | YES |
|----|-----|

*You worked hard on those decorations! Show them off by **composing a closeup shot** of you and your backdrop.*

## USING PROPS

| NO | YES |
|----|-----|

*Don't overdo it. **Pick a few elements** to include in the shot and use the remaining space to capture your guests having a great time.*

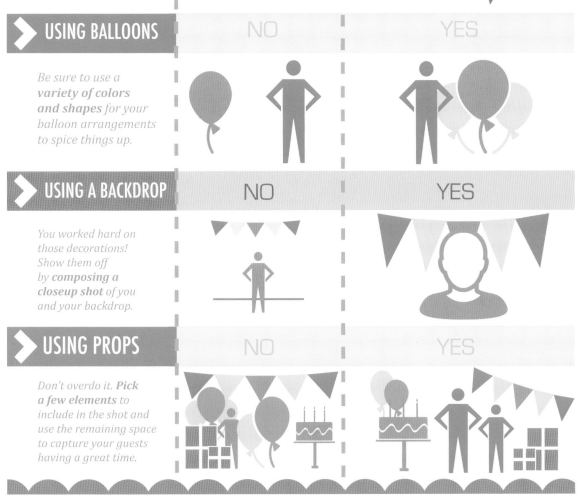

# MENU SELECTION

*chapter eight*

Your child's birthday party only comes around once a year but is a special opportunity for you to lavish attention on those adorable little kiddies that you love. But a birthday party for your little one can have a fast-growing tab as you line up fun activities, pricey venues, extravagant decorations, well-known entertainers, custom cakes, and exquisite parting gifts in favor bags. A great party doesn't mean that it has to come at a great cost, though. Luckily, if you raised them right, most kids are pleased with the simple things for their party. If you've covered all of the basics, the party can be a hit without being expensive—especially when it comes to the birthday menu. This is especially true if your birthday party is for your son, because he is more likely to be happy with the most basic food as opposed to the daughter who may have more dietary requests than her brother.

Keeping the food budget under control is one of the easiest ways to keep the cost of hosting a kid's birthday party simple and affordable. Let's create the menu. When it comes to the menu, the best place to start is with what the guest of honor would like to eat at his or her party. If the party is for a younger child, then there is less chance that he or she will ask for anything too elaborate or gourmet. The entrées requested will probably consist of the quintessential kids' foods like pizza, burgers, and hot dogs—all of which are relatively cheap. When creating your grocery list for the party, note which items can be bought in bulk or at a big-box warehouse store like Costco or Sam's Club. Individually-packaged items such as pretzels, graham crackers, Popsicles, and even juice boxes are often much more expensive than their respective economy-sized counterparts.

If you will be preparing the food for the party, you may want to consider limiting the guest list to a handful of close friends. This has an added benefit in that it is another way to save time and money. The shorter guest list makes it easier to guarantee that there will be plenty of food, drinks, and snacks to go around. Also, whether you are preparing the food or not, you should check with the parents to see if there are any food allergies that you need to be aware of. The risk of allergies is higher with shrimp and crab than pizza, but you should still check. And when it comes to dessert, if you're planning to serve cake and ice cream, you should steer clear of nuts as well. Remember that the food should add to the theme, add an element of fun, and add to the excitement and anticipation for the kids but not add stress to the host or hostess of the birthday party.

QUICK TIP
Wait until dessert to place
the cup & saucer

## FORMAL PLACE SETTING

Everything about a formal table should be about placement and appear geometrically spaced: the centerpiece at the exact center; the place settings equally balanced and utensils placed equally apart. Creative elements can be added after this basic structure.

## WHAT YOU'LL NEED

1. Napkin
2. Bread Plate
3. Place Card
4. Salad Fork
5. Dinner Fork
6. Service Plate
7. Salad Plate
8. Cake Fork

9. Dessert Spoon
10. Water Glass
11. Wineglass (red)
12. Wineglass (white)
13. Dinner Knife
14. Teaspoon
15. Soup Spoon
16. Cup & Saucer

# Table Setting

**QUICK TIP**

Set your spread 1 inch
from the table's edge

The practice of dictating the precise arrangement of tableware can vary across cultures and history. The two basic structures of formal and informal will fit any event you're planning depending on style appropriately.

*INFORMAL PLACE SETTING*: When an informal three-course dinner is served, the typical place setting includes these utensils and dishes if you are serving. Buffet it is the same without the plate.

## WHAT YOU'LL NEED

1. Salad Fork
2. Dinner Fork
3. Napkin
4. Plate
5. Dinner Knife
6. Teaspoon
7. Soup Spoon
8. Water Glass
9. Wineglass

## NOTE ABOUT PLACE SETTINGS

When you are hosting a child's party for kids under ten you usually have a buffet-style meal or the eating is usually very casual, if not for the sheer fact that young kids don't sit still long. When hosting for your tween, sometimes a more formal party like a tea party or family gathering require place setting. I have created an informal and a formal place setting guide that you might feel is useful for these occasions.

Below are some of my favorite kid-friendly finger foods, party drinks, food on a stick, dips and mixes, and party themed food stations.

KIDS PARTY DRINKS

### GUMMY BEAR SODA

Kids love gummy bears. Okay—you caught me—so do adults. So, here is a cute party drink that will please the young and the young at heart. It's so simple to mix up.

*Ingredients:*

**SPRITE OR 7-UP**

**GUMMY BEARS**

**GRENADINE (OPTIONAL)**

*Directions:*

For this drink, you simply arrange the gummy bears in the glass the way you want them and then pour the 7-Up or Sprite over them for a sweet and fun colorful drink. I like to add a little grenadine first so it stays at the bottom of the glass for a new spin on a Shirley Temple taste. Another fun way to use this same concept is to create gummy bear ice cubes in a large ice cube tray and Sprite, or make gummy bear popsicles at home, just fill the Popsicle molds with gummy bears. Then pour in the soda and freeze for about 4 hours and enjoy.

## ROCK CANDY QUENCHER

This is a fun way to make your child's party feel more sophisticated. I love to use long, pretty glasses for this one. I found the rock candy at my local Party City but you can also find it online in many colors. This is such a fun, non-alcoholic drink for kids, and is perfect for your New Year's celebrations.

*Ingredients:*

**CANADA DRY GINGER ALE**

**ROCK CANDY ON A STICK**

*Directions:*

Simply add one rock candy on a stick to each of your serving glasses; my "Serve It Pretty" advice is to line them up on a tray or nicely line them up in a grouping on your serving table. Keep your ginger ale in the refrigerator and add as requested; however you serve it, you will want to serve them immediately after you add the liquid.

## GUMMY FISH FIZZ

What is better than a day at the beach? At a little fishing party, this fun drink is always a winner and will never leave your kids sad. I will never forget the sight of my son's ear-to-ear smile when I served these up randomly for dinner one night. Not just the fun blue liquid filling the cup to the brim, but also the candy fish make it magical for kids of all ages.

*Ingredients:*

*Directions:*

**3 TBSP. WATER**

**3 TBSP. SUGAR IN THE RAW**

**1 TSP. COCONUT EXTRACT**

**3 DROPS BLUE FOOD COLORING**

**2 CANS OF 7-UP**

In a small microwave-safe bowl, combine water and sugar. Heat in microwave for about 1 minute. Stir until sugar is completely dissolved.

Pour the sugar mixture into a pitcher. Add coconut extract, food coloring, and soda. Stir to combine. "Serve It Pretty" over ice with a fish on a stick garnish.

## RAINBOW ICE WATER

This is fun, easy, and a perfect accent to any rainbow party.

*Ingredients:*

*Directions:*

**WATER**

**WILTON® LIQUID FOOD COLORING**

I just make red, orange, yellow, green, blue, and purple ice cubes using basic Wilton® food coloring. Put the ice cube trays in the freeze and in no time at all you have colored ice. Yes, I know this one is totally basic, but I had to include it; you can have so much fun with ice cubes add edible flowers, use fun shape ice cube trays, bits of fruit, or even use juice or 7-Up instead of water. The sky is the limit.

## RED HOT SHIRLEY

This drink is a hit at every party, so why not completely spoil the kids with a stick of cherries? They will go crazy for this and the Red Hots add a little kick to every sip.

*Ingredients:*

**ICE**

**4 TBSP. GRENADINE**

**1 CAN 7-UP**

**3 TBSP. CANDY RED HOTS**

**MARASCHINO CHERRIES, PILED HIGH ON A SKEWER**

*Directions:*

Mix together the ice, grenadine, and 7-Up, then add in the Red Hots and maraschino cherries as desired.

*Quick and Easy Alternative*

Use your favorite vintage bottled Shirley Temple and add a scoop of Red Hots

## THE ORIGINAL SHIRLEY TEMPLE

This sweet classic is an easy pleaser for kids and adults.

*Ingredients:*

**ICE**

**1 TBSP. GRENADINE**

**1 CUP SPRITE OR GINGER ALE**

**1 MARASCHINO CHERRY**

*Directions:*

In a tall glass, add ice, grenadine, and lemon-lime soda. Mix together.

"Serve It Pretty" in a tall glass with a cherry skewer flagged with a printable or sticker.

## JELLY BELLY FRUIT TEA

Bubble and Jelly Tea are all the rage! You can infuse flavors into jasmine or green tea with purchased tea syrup or nectar juices; the juice or syrup will add body and a hint of sweetness to your fun Jelly drink. The jelly gives you the feeling of biting into the real fruit

*Ingredients:*

**¼ CUP JELLY CUBES PURCHASED AT AN ASIAN MARKET OR ONLINE FROM BUDDHA BUBBLES BOBA**

**1½ CUP WATER**

**2 JASMINE OR GREEN TEA BAGS (I LIKE TO USE REPUBLIC OF TEA BRAND)**

**½ CUP SUGAR (SUGAR IN THE RAW BRAND)**

**FRUIT JUICE OR JUICE NECTAR IS OPTIONAL**

*Directions:*

Make a strong cup of tea. Boil 1½ cups of water, remove from heat, and add 2 tea bags; let steep for about 15 minutes and then chill the tea. Add the mango fruit nectar and sugar together. When the sugar has dissolved, add it to the tea and then add your jelly. "Serve It Pretty" with a wide straw for sucking up the yummy jelly pieces.

## COTTON CANDY MOCKTAIL

Cotton candy and Pellegrino seltzer water are all you need for this crowd pleaser—a young crowd pleaser, that is. You can get cotton candy from the dollar store or from Walmart in a tub. The brighter the color of the cotton candy, the more fun it is to watch as it dissolves. Kids love this drink as they watch the clear liquid change color and the full glass of cotton candy fluff dissolve.

*Ingredients:*

**PRE-MADE COTTON CANDY**

**PELLEGRINO SELTZER WATER**

*Directions:*

Fill glass high with the cotton candy.

Pour the Pellegrino seltzer water over cotton candy slowly and watch it dissolve and the liquid change colors.

# BUBBLE BOBA DELIGHT

I live in California, where boba tea is all the rage, and it is spreading across the county in hundreds of drink and recipes. Boba tea originated in Taiwan in the 1980s and became popular in Asia before finding its way to the USA. You can find boba at almost any Asian grocery store. If you don't have one down the street, you can find all types online. What is boba? They are small, colorful balls made from tapioca, and they come in all sorts of colors and sizes. Some of them can cook up bland, so I like to soak mine in simple syrup. You want your boba to be sweet and chewy. I "Serve It Pretty" in clear glasses that are narrower at the bottom than at the top so you can really see the boba stand out. You can also find boba straws online; kids love to suck the boba up through the straw.

## Ingredients:

¼ CUP DRIED BOBA TAPIOCA PEARLS PER SERVING— DO NOT USE A QUICK-COOK BOBA

1-2 TEA BAGS PER SERVING, USE A FRUIT TEA FOR KIDS (I RECOMMEND REPUBLIC OF TEA BRAND)

1½ CUPS OF WATER

½ CUP SUGAR (SUGAR IN THE RAW BRAND)

FAIR LIFE WHOLE MILK, ALMOND MILK, OR CARNATION SWEETENED CONDENSED MILK

FRUIT JUICE OR JUICE NECTAR IS OPTIONAL

SAUCEPAN

## Directions:

Make a strong cup of tea by boiling 1½ cups of water; remove from heat and add 2 tea bags. Let tea steep for about 15 minutes and then chill the tea.

Cook the Boba: Be sure to cook ¼ cup of boba for every 2 cups of water. Boil water on high and then slowly stir in the boba. When they start to float to the top of the water, you can turn the heat down to medium. Cook for about 13 minutes, then remove from the heat and let it sit for 15 minutes until boba is soft but still firm.

Prepare Simple Syrup for Soaking the Boba: While the boba are cooking, make a homemade, simple sugar syrup using sugar in the raw. This syrup will sweeten and preserve the boba after you cook them. Boil ½ cup of water and stir in ½ cup sugar and stir until dissolved. Set aside to cool. And just like that, you just made Simple Syrup. It's great to make a batch of this and use it as a liquid sweetener for your drinks and cooking.

When you have finished cooking the boba, drain them and put them in a small bowl or container. Then, fully submerge the boba in your simple syrup. Let them soak for 15 minutes. To cool them, you can put them in the fridge for later use or until you're ready to use them.

Combine all the tea, milk, and/or juice in a cocktail shaker with ice cubes and shake for 15 seconds. Pour into a tall glass and add the boba.

## LAYERED DRINKS

You can stop chasing rainbows and just make one yourself. The trick to magical layered drinks is the sugar content in the beverages. You can make beautiful layered drinks in any color just as long as the drink with the heaviest sugar content goes in first and then then graduate them down in their sugar content. This drink was made from a Strawberry Quencher, a Sobe White Pina Colada drink, and a V8 Splash. When you want super clean lines between your layers, you can use a tool called the Final Touch® Rainbow Cocktail™ Layering Tool: this will help you combine each layer. Drinks have never looked so beautiful and you will feel like a drink alchemist.

## SUNRISE SMILES

This drink is a classic in my family; we've had it at Sunday brunch since I was a kid. I love making them for my kids as a family tradition—maybe it will become part of yours.

*Ingredients:*

### 1 GLASS ORANGE JUICE

### ABOUT 4 TBSP. GRENADINE (OR UNTIL YOU GET THE RIGHT EFFECT IN YOUR GLASS)

*Directions:*

Use a tall glass with ice, topping the ice with orange juice. Stir it up and add grenadine by pouring grenadine directly down the side of the glass very quickly. The grenadine should go straight to the bottom because of its high sugar content and then should rise up slowly through the drink creating a beautiful sunset effect. "Serve It Pretty" with cherries and orange.

## BLUEBERRY LEMONADE

At a sweet picnic party or BBQ, I love to throw in a few of the squeezed lemon rinds into lemonade to give some zing and a burst of flavor.

*Ingredients:*

½ CUP FRESH LEMON JUICE

4 CUPS WATER

1 CUP SIMPLE SYRUP

½ CUP BLUEBERRIES

*Directions:*

In a decanter or pitcher, combine lemon juice, water, and simple syrup. Add blueberries and lemon slices and "Serve It Pretty" with a fun party straw.

## SIMPLE SYRUP

You can use this syrup in anything you would use sugar for: hot tea, cereal, pancakes, or to drizzle on a muffin or over strawberries.

*Ingredients:*

2 CUPS WATER

1½ CUPS SUGAR

½ CUPS LIGHT CORN SYRUP

*Directions:*

Use a medium sauce pan and combine all ingredients. Heat on medium, stirring consistently until the sugar has dissolved for 20 seconds and it looks well mixed. Let cool and chill before adding. This makes about 3 cups. I love to keep it in a mason jar in the refrigerator and use it for all sorts of things.

## CHOCOLATE SHAKE GELATO SHAKE

Sometimes we love to indulge and what better way to do so than a homemade premium gelato shake? Yes, I am serious. Gelato makes the best shakes ever. Follow my simple recipe and "Serve It Pretty" and I guarantee you your kids will flip for this treat.

*Ingredients:*

**1 PINT TALENTI CHOCOLATE GELATO**

**4 MINI CHOCOLATE CUPCAKES**

**⅓ CUP OF WHOLE FAIRLIFE MILK**

**2 TSP. OF NATURAL CHOCOLATE SPRINKLES**

*Directions:*

Throw it all in a blender and it's just that easy! I like to make the kids go crazy for them by "Serving It Pretty"—covering the glass rims with Nutella and dipping them in the chocolate sprinkles.

# NOAH'S HORCHATA

## Ingredients:

**1 CINNAMON STICK**

**4 CUPS FAIRLIFE WHOLE MILK**

**1 CAN OR 14 OZ. OF CARNATION® SWEETENED CONDENSED MILK**

**½ CUP RICE OR ALMOND FLOUR (I PREFER TO USE BOB'S RED MILL FLOUR)**

**2 TSP. PURE VANILLA EXTRACT**

**ICE CUBES**

**GROUND CINNAMON AND CINNAMON STICKS TO GARNISH**

## Directions:

First, put the cinnamon stick in the milk and bring to a simmer over medium heat. Remove from heat. Pour the milk into a tempered medium-sized mixing bowl and use a whisk to mix in the flour, condensed milk, and vanilla extract. Then put it in the fridge to chill for 30 minutes. When it is thoroughly chilled, you will want to use a fine sieve to strain the mixture; then it's ready for serving. I like to "Serve It Pretty" by using short, wide glasses and serving the horchata over ice, and garnishing with ground cinnamon and a cinnamon stick.

## CROC GUAC

Makes 8–10 servings

### Ingredients:

**4 RIPE AVOCADOS, SEEDLESS AND DICED.**

**2 RIPE RED TOMATOES, DICED**

**2 JALAPEÑO PEPPERS**

**1 TSP. GARLIC SALT**

**2½ (19-OZ.) CAN OF BLACK BEANS, DRAINED AND RINSED**

**4 GREEN ONIONS, THINLY SLICED**

**2 LIMES, JUICED**

**½ CUP OF SHARP CHEDDAR CHEESE, GRATED**

### Directions:

Place two of the avocados in a bowl. Add the tomatoes, jalapeño peppers, garlic salt, and lime juice. Mash lightly with a potato masher. Add beans, onions, and cheese, along with the two remaining avocados. Stir to combine. Chill until ready to use. Serve with tortilla chips.

## CIRCUS CAKE BATTER COOKIE DIP

Makes 8 servings

Milk, cream cheese, powdered sugar, and oil-free cake batter and that is it. You just need 4 ingredients (plus sprinkles!) for this seemingly sinful dessert dip!

### Ingredients:

**4 OZ. PHILADELPHIA CREAM CHEESE, SOFTENED TO ROOM TEMPERATURE**

**1½ CUP PILLSBURY® FUNFETTI CAKE MIX**

**6 TBSP. MILK (I LIKE TO USE FAIRLIFE WHOLE MILK)**

**¾ CUP POWDERED SUGAR**

**⅓ CUP SPRINKLES TO MIX IN YOUR DIP AND FOR DECORATING**

### Directions:

First, beat the cream cheese on medium-high speed until it's smooth and you don't see any remaining lumps. Reduce the speed of your mixer to low and slowly spoon in the Funfetti cake mix and the milk evenly, alternating between the cake mix and the milk. Mix in the cake mix completely.

Reduce mixer speed again to low and add the powdered sugar. Increase mixer to medium speed and blend until completely combined.

Slowly stir in your colorful sprinkles with a mini spatula and you're ready to serve. I love to "Serve It Pretty" with classic animal crackers, graham crackers, pretzels, or even fruit.

## DOLLY'S ORIGINAL FRUIT DIP

Makes 8–10

This one is so easy to make everyone thinks I am kidding when I give them the recipe. My mom used to make this for everything from family events to my weekend sleepovers and all my friends would eat it up. She used to call it liquid cheesecake but I call it "Dolly's Original Fruit Dip" in honor of my late mom.

### Ingredients:

**1 (8-OZ.) PACKAGE OF PHILADELPHIA CREAM CHEESE**

**1 (7-OZ.) CONTAINER JET-PUFFED MARSHMALLOW CREME**

**½ TSP. FULL OF WHITE SUGAR**

**1 TSP. ORANGE ZEST**

**1 TSP. FINELY GRATED ORANGE PEEL**

**1 FLAT OF STRAWBERRIES**

**½ CUP ORANGE JUICE**

### Directions:

This recipe will blow you away it's so easy. Just add the softened cream cheese and marshmallow creme together in a bowl and mix to desired consistency. Add the sugar and orange zest. Sprinkle in the peel and mix thoroughly—it should appear speckled. Chill and it's ready to serve

For the ultimate treat, prep your strawberries like this: remove the stems, put in a bowl, and cover them with the orange juice and sugar. Sometimes I like to add the zest to the strawberries. Zest is strips or thin layers of the orange peel. Cover and chill then serve strawberries and dip together.

## CRAZY COTTON CANDY DIP

This dip is so easy to make it's crazy! That's why I like to call it crazy cotton candy dip. I love to serve it with butter cookies, pita chips, pretzels, or bread sticks. Another fun thing to do it spread on white bread and roll around a banana. Kids LOVE this one!

*Ingredients:*

**1 CUP HEAVY WHIPPING CREAM**

**2 OZ. PINK OR BLUE COTTON CANDY**

**1 (8-OZ.) PACKAGE OF PHILADELPHIA CREAM CHEESE, SOFTENED TO ROOM TEMPERATURE**

**½ CUP POWDERED SUGAR**

**GEL FOOD COLORING FOR A BRIGHT STAND-OUT DIP, IF YOU WANT AN EXTRA SPLASH OF COLOR**

*Directions:*

First, pour the heavy whipping cream into a bowl and add in the cotton candy. The cotton candy will automatically dissolve. Then beat the cream with a mixer until soft peaks form.

In a separate bowl, mix the cream cheese and powdered sugar together until it's nice and smooth. Fold in the whipped cream mixture and then chill. If you want to add in the food coloring, just add a couple drops until you get the color you want before refrigerating for 45 minutes or until it cools.

# GET LUCKY PARTY CHEX MIX

## *Ingredients:*

**1 BOX LUCKY CHARMS CEREAL**

**6 CUPS RICE CHEX™ OR CORN CHEX™ CEREAL (I LIKE THE RICE CHEX™; IT'S BEST FOR THIS MIX)**

**2 (12-OZ.) BAGS OF WHITE VANILLA CHOCOLATE CHIPS**

**¼ CUP MULTICOLORED CANDY SPRINKLES**

## *Directions:*

Pour the box of Lucky Charms cereal out onto a large tray. Pick out all the marshmallows (2 cups); set aside to add to the mix later. Measure 2 cups of the remaining Lucky Charms cereal (without the marshmallows) into large bowl and add Chex™ cereal.

Line cookie sheet with foil or waxed paper. In a medium microwavable bowl, microwave white vanilla baking chips uncovered on high for 2 minutes, stirring every 30 seconds, until chips are melted and smooth. Pour over cereal mixture in large bowl; toss to evenly coat.

Spread mixture in a single layer on cookie sheet. Immediately sprinkle with candy sprinkles. Let stand for 20 minutes, or until set. Gently break up mixture and toss in reserved marshmallows. Store in airtight container.

## LEMONADE CHEX™ MIX

This party mix is perfect to serve at a lemonade party or to sell at your lemonade stand. It's easy to make and fun to eat. A bit of bitter with a lemony sweet makes for a treat you just can't stop eating.

### WARNING: MAY BECOME ADDICTIVE.

*Ingredients:*

1½ CUPS WHITE CHOCOLATE CHIPS

¼ CUP HORIZONS UNSALTED BUTTER

4 TSP. LEMON ZEST AND PEEL

2 TBSP. LEMON JUICE

9 CUPS RICE CHEX™

2 CUPS POWDERED SUGAR

*Directions:*

In a saucepan, combine the chocolate, butter, lemon zest, and lemon juice and melt over a medium heat. Continually stir until it is all combined and melted.

Remove from the heat and pour directly over your cereal and stir gently, being careful not to be too hard on the cereal—you don't want broken cereal pieces. You want to stir until all the Chex™ pieces are coated evenly.

The last step is to pour the chocolate-covered cereal into a large ziplock bag; I use a 1-gallon bag for mixing. Add the powdered sugar and shake it until you cover all the cereal evenly. Pour it into a bowl and garnish with the lemon rind or "Serve It Pretty" by separating it into little single serving cups or treat bags with a lemonade printable (available for free on www.ILovePartyStyle.com).

# BIRTHDAY CAKE SNACK MIX

*Ingredients:*

½ CUP ORGANIC POPCORN KERNELS

2 BAGS OF WILTON WHITE, VANILLA-FLAVORED CANDY MELTS®

½ CUP YELLOW CAKE MIX

1 (8-OZ.) BAG OF M&M'S® CANDY

12 CLASSIC OREO COOKIES, BROKEN INTO PIECES

BRIGHTLY COLORED SPRINKLES

*Directions:*

I only use organic popcorn made in an air popper; air poppers are surprisingly cheap and a great investment. Pop the popcorn kernels and remove any stray seeds so you don't chip a tooth while enjoying your snack.

Lay out two baking sheets and cover in wax paper

Melt your Wilton® candy melts—I like to use the Wilton® candy melting pot for this because it melts perfectly every time. Next, stir in your dry cake mix until it's completely mixed.

Now you will want to work quickly because your candy will begin to harden. Pour the candy melts over your popcorn and thoroughly mix it. Add in your M&M's® and OREO pieces and continue mixing until they are slightly covered with candy also.

Divide and spread your mix over the two baking sheets. Shake sprinkles all over the popcorn before it hardens. After it stiffens, break into pieces, and you can "Serve It Pretty" in a bowl or in treat cups with a fun 2-inch birthday mix printable. Printable is available at www.ILovePartyStyle.com.

## WORLD'S BEST HOT CHOCOLATE CHEESECAKE DIP

Makes about 2 cups.

### Ingredients:

**1 (8-OZ.) PACKAGE OF PHILADELPHIA CREAM CHEESE**

**½ CUP PLAIN CHOBANI® GREEK YOGURT**

**½ CUP JET-PUFFED MARSHMALLOW CREME**

**1 CUP POWDERED SWISS MISS DARK SENSATION HOT CHOCOLATE MIX**

**¾ CUP COOL WHIP**

**MINI JET-PUFFED MARSHMALLOWS FOR GARNISH**

**CHOCOLATE SPRINKLES, CANDY CANES, AND MINI CHIPS FOR GARNISHING**

**FUN FOODS FOR DIPPING**

### Directions:

Beat the cream cheese until creamy. Add the yogurt, marshmallow creme, and hot chocolate mix and beat again until light and fluffy. Fold in ½ cup Cool Whip gently until completely mixed in.

Top with remaining Cool Whip, mini marshmallows, and crushed candy cane.

Serve with cookies and pretzels. Keep refrigerated in a covered container.

# CAMP OUT CHEX™ PARTY MIX

This mix has a little bit of everything and is completely indulgent for children and adults. This one will have the neighbors asking for the recipe. I personally find this mix perfect for sporting events, camping, and outdoor parties.

## Ingredients:

**8 CUPS CHOCOLATE CHEX™ CEREAL**

**¾ CUP BROWN SUGAR**

**6 TBSP. BUTTER**

**3 TBSP. LIGHT CORN SYRUP**

**¼ TSP. BAKING SODA**

**1 CUP MINI REESE'S® PEANUT BUTTER CUPS**

**1 CUP MINI JET-PUFFED MARSHMALLOWS**

**½ CUP CARAMEL PIECES**

**1 TBSP. HEAVY CREAM (I LIKE TO USE STRAUSS FAMILY FARM CREAMERY)**

**½ CUP CHOCOLATE BAKING CHIPS**

**½ CUP WHITE CHOCOLATE BAKING CHIPS**

**1 TSP. SEA SALT**

## Directions:

Okay, let the fun begin! Put the cereal in a large bowl and set it aside.

Line 2 cookie sheets with wax paper and set those aside.

Add the brown sugar, butter, and corn syrup in a microwavable cup and heat on high for 2 minutes, checking on it and giving it a stir after the first minute. When it is melted and smooth, stir in the baking soda until dissolved. Working quickly, pour the mixture over the cereal and start to stir it until all the cereal is totally covered with the caramel mixture. Cool for 10 minutes, then break into bite-sized pieces.

Once the mixture is cool, add in the mini peanut butter cups candy and miniature marshmallows. Be sure the Chex™ mixture is cool to the touch or the candy will melt when it's added.

In small microwavable bowl, microwave the caramel pieces and cream on high for 1 minute. You want it to be smooth and melted, so add more time if necessary. Simply use a spoon and drizzle over the mix. Next, melt the milk chocolate baking chips in a small saucepan, stirring until completely smooth. Drizzle over the snack mixture. Repeat the process with white baking chips until smooth, and then drizzle that over the mixture before it hardens quickly. Sprinkle coarse salt over mixture while candy drizzles are still wet. Put into the fridge for a quick hardening. When hardened, remove it from the fridge; break it into pieces, and "Serve It Pretty" in single serving glass bowl for an indulgent treat. Add a name tag or a quote tag for a styled touch. Tags and signs can be downloaded for free on www.ILovePartyStyle.com

## RITZY PARTY DIP

*Ingredients:*

**5-6 GREEN ONIONS**

**8 OZ. CHEDDAR CHEESE, SHREDDED (I LIKE TO USE FRESHLY GRATED CHEESE BUT KRAFT SHREDDED MEXICAN BLEND IS GOOD TOO)**

**1½ CUPS BEST FOODS® MAYONNAISE, OR FOR VEGAN OPTION, USE HAMPTON CREEK JUST MAYO**

**½ LB. OF BACON, COOKED TO A CRISP AND PIECED, OR 1 JAR HORMEL REAL BACON BITS**

**1 PKG. SLIVERED ALMONDS**

*Directions:*

Chop the green onions. Shred the cheddar cheese. Piece the bacon.

Mix the onions, cheese, mayo, bacon bits, and slivered almonds together.

Chill for a couple hours. Best served with classic Ritz crackers for kids' parties, but it is also good with a variety of crackers and chips, even veggies. I love it with Ritz, so that's why I call it the Ritzy Party dip.

## FAIRY BREAD PINWHEELS

Australia is always creating new party trends; if you are planning a kid's party and you live in the land down under, then chances are that you are serving up a fun version of fairy bread. Kids LOVE it! I guarantee that fairy bread will be a go-to for everything: from a slumber party snack to full-blown holiday soirées, this one will end up making its way to the kids table every time, mainly because of how totally easy and versatile it is.

So what is in fairy bread, you ask?

### Ingredients:

**WHITE BREAD**

**HORIZON® ORGANIC SALTED BUTTER**

**WHITE SUGAR**

**CANDY SPRINKLES**

**CHOCOLATE SPRINKLES**

### Directions:

Get creative with your fairy bread creations. I like to roll mine, so cut the crust off your white bread, spread lightly with butter, sprinkle about 1 tablespoon of white sugar, dip sides in sprinkles, and roll them up and secure with a toothpick. I love to serve these little gems pretty by adding flags or mini honeycombs to my toothpicks and lining them up on single serving trays.

Typically, the bread is cut into squares or triangles . . . but, as this has been done so many times before, why not be a bit creative and make hearts, shamrocks, or butterfly wings?

ON-A-STICK FOODS

## SALAD ON A STICK

### Ingredients:

**1 CUCUMBER, THINLY SLICED**

**2 CARROTS, THINLY SLICED**

**½ HEAD ICEBERG LETTUCE, CUT INTO 2½-INCH CHUNKS**

**1 CUP GRAPE OR CHERRY TOMATOES**

**BLUE CHEESE DRESSING FOR SERVING**

### Directions:

Fun and easy! Just thread the cucumber, carrots, lettuce, and mini cherry tomatoes onto 6-inch-long wooden skewers, alternating the vegetables. Refrigerate and serve with the dressing.

# BACON BURGER ON A STICK

## Ingredients:

**4 PIECES OF FLAT BREAD**

**ICEBERG LETTUCE**

**SLICED CHEESE (I PREFER CHEDDAR OR PEPPER JACK)**

**CHERRY TOMATOES**

**BACON STRIPS**

**1 LB. GROUND BEEF**

**1 TSP. GARLIC SALT**

**1½ TBSP. WORCESTERSHIRE SAUCE**

**MAYONNAISE**

**BBQ SAUCE OR KETCHUP**

**THICK PARTY SKEWERS**

## Directions:

Start by cutting little, round 2-inch pieces of bread, using a round cookie cutter or the top of your garlic salt lid. You'll need 2 circle pieces per Bacon Burger Skewer. Next, cut the lettuce into squares—try to cut everything around the same size. Then cut the cheese into pieces. I like to use a block cheese so it looks kind of rustic. Cut your cherry tomatoes into halves with a sharp knife.

First, fry up your bacon so it's nice and crispy, then cut it into about 1½-inch pieces. Do not cut it before frying because it will shrink while cooking and be way too small. For the burgers, season your ground beef as you regularly would; I always use Lawry's garlic salt, Worcestershire sauce, and ground black pepper.

Roll your seasoned ground beef into little meatballs and flatten them to be the same size as your bread cutouts. Press a little divot into the center: this will help them not shrink to much as you cook them. Pan fry them for a couple minutes and they should be ready for serving.

Now, assemble your bacon burger on a stick. Start with a piece of bread and add a little mayo, then a couple of pieces of lettuce, a piece of bacon, a burger (first dipped in some BBQ sauce), then a slice of cheese, another piece of bread, and top it off with a cherry tomato half. "Serve It Pretty" by sticking the skewers in a tall glass or using a half melon to stick them in and serve.

# ANTHONY'S SPAGHETTI & MEATBALL STICK

Makes 64 Spaghetti & Meatball Sticks.

## Ingredients:

**2 CUPS FRESH BASIL LEAVES, PACKED**

**1 TSP. FRESH OREGANO**

**1 TSP. FRESH PARSLEY**

**2 CLOVES GARLIC**

**¼ CUP PINE NUTS**

**⅔ CUP EXTRA-VIRGIN OLIVE OIL, DIVIDED**

**PINK HIMALAYAN SALT OR SEA SALT**

**PEPPER, TO TASTE**

**1 LB. OF THICK SPAGHETTI PASTA**

**EXTRA VIRGIN OLIVE OIL (EVOO) OR OLIVE OIL NON-STICK COOKING SPRAY**

**2 LBS. OF PACKAGED COOKED MEATBALLS (½-OZ. EACH), HEATED ACCORDING TO PACKAGE DIRECTIONS**

**64 BAMBOO SKEWERS**

**½ CUP PECORINO ROMANO CHEESE, GRATED**

**1½ CUPS MARINARA SAUCE**

## Directions:

Combine the basil, oregano, parsley, garlic, and pine nuts in a food processor and pulse blend until coarsely chopped. Next, add the ½ cup of oil and continue to process until it is fully incorporated and smooth. Season with salt and pepper.

Add the remaining oil and pulse until smooth. Transfer the pesto to a large serving bowl and mix in the cheese.

Pecorino Romano was a staple in the diet for the legionaries of ancient Rome. Pecorino Romano is a hard, salty Italian cheese, made out of sheep's milk and is often used for grating. However, the American counterpart of the cheese is made from cow's milk. As an alternative, you can use Parmesan cheese in place of the Pecorino Romano.

Cook pasta to al dente according to directions:

Bring 4–6 quarts of water to a rolling boil and add salt to taste. Add pasta to boiling water. Stir gently. Return to a boil. For authentic "al dente" pasta, boil uncovered, stirring occasionally for 12 minutes. Remove from heat. Drain well.

Brush drained pasta with EVOO or spray olive oil non-stick cooking spray. Set aside.

Preheat oven to 180°F. Place meatballs on rimmed, lightly oiled baking sheet.

Working with 3 or 4 strands, twirl pasta around a skewer. Stick each completed skewer into a meatball. Repeat until all meatballs are skewered. Brush completed spaghetti-and-meatball skewers with EVOO or spray with non-stick olive oil spray. Bake 5 to 7 minutes to "set" pasta.

Meanwhile, choose a flat platter for serving.

Place pesto in a squeeze bottle with a large opening. Paint the platter, using a simple pattern of stripes or swirls.

Using a teaspoon, make a few circles of marinara sauce over the pesto on the platter. Place a warmed spaghetti-and-meatball skewer on each circle of sauce.

Thick spaghetti pairs well with just about any kind of marinara sauce as well as oil-based and cream-based sauces.

Makes about 64 Spaghetti and Meatballs on a Stick.

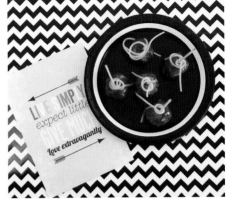

## FRUIT KABOBS

*Ingredients:*

**6 CUPS BITE-SIZE PIECES ASSORTED FRESH FRUIT (PINEAPPLE, WATERMELON, HONEYDEW MELON, AND CANTALOUPE)**

**1 CUP GREEN GRAPES**

**1 CUP BLUEBERRIES**

**1 CUP RED GRAPES**

**1 CUP MARASCHINO CHERRIES**

**3-4 SMALL CARAMBOLA, CUT INTO 24 SLICES**

**2 LARGE MANGOS, PEELED, SEEDS REMOVED, AND CUT INTO LARGE PIECES**

**¼ CUP PINEAPPLE PRESERVES**

*Directions:*

Thread 4 to 6 pieces of fruits (except mangos) on each of twenty-four 6-inch skewers. Place skewers on large serving platter; set aside.

Create the mango purée. In food processor, place mango pieces and pineapple preserves. Cover and process until smooth; pour into small serving bowl. Serve the fruit kabobs with the mango purée.

## CANDY SKEWERS

Candy Skewers are super easy and make for a fun activity to do at a birthday party! All you need are bamboo skewers and a variety of gummy candy and soft candies. Let your kids help create this treat for your party as they choose which candy to add to the skewers. You can also create skewers to give out at the end of the party as favors. Have the kids wrap the skewers in a cellophane bag tied with ribbon.

*Ingredients:*

1 CUP OF GUMMY BEARS

1 CUP OF SWEDISH FISH

1 CUP OF JELLY BEANS

12 FRUIT ROLLUPS CUT INTO SQUARES

1 CUP OF GUMMY WORMS

1 CUP OF ORANGE SLICES CANDIES

1 (16-OZ.) PACKAGE OF CHERRY TWIZZLERS BITES

1 CUP GUMMY SHARKS

*Directions:*

Simply slide candy down a skewer, alternating candy types and colors, and keep stacking until the skewer is full. Choose colored candy to match party colors or the party theme and watch the kids smile ear to ear as they snack on a candy skewers!

# STRAWBERRY SHORTCAKE ON A STICK

*Ingredients:*

**STORE BOUGHT OR HOMEMADE POUND CAKE OR ANGEL FOOD CAKE, CUT INTO CUBES**

**SMALL FRESH STRAWBERRIES (GREEN STEMS REMOVED)**

**MIDSIZED SKEWERS**

**WHIPPED TOPPING OR FRESHLY WHIPPED CREAM**

**BLUEBERRIES, OPTIONAL**

**POWDERED SUGAR**

*Directions:*

String cake with strawberries and cake, then whipped cream. Place onto skewers. Place on a platter and sprinkle with powdered sugar and serve with blueberries. Serve with a bowl of extra whipped cream.

*Ingredients:*

## WILTON CANDY MELTS® OR CHOCOLATE CHIPS

## BANANAS

## MINI JET-PUFFED MARSHMALLOWS

## ASSORTED CRUSHED NUTS

## M&M'S®

## SPRINKLES

## COCONUT OIL

*Directions:*

Place the chocolate in a Wilton® candy melter bowl. Let the chocolate melt, stirring occasionally, until the chocolate is completely melted.

While the chocolate is melting, prepare the bananas and toppings by peeling the bananas and then slicing the bananas into ½-inch slices. Pour the toppings into the bowls.

Add the coconut oil to the chocolate and stir until completely combined. The coconut oil will help loosen the chocolate and make a thinner coat over the bananas.

Dip the banana slices into the chocolate one at a time using a skewer. Make sure to dunk the banana completely into the chocolate and coat it entirely. Lift the slice out with your skewer and slightly tap it against the inside of the melter bowl to remove excess chocolate.

Coat the banana slice with toppings. Use a pinch of toppings with your fingers to sprinkle additional sprinkles coating over the top of the banana slice.

Transfer the banana slice to the baking sheet by using your bamboo skewer; stab the banana slice and lift it out of the toppings. Transfer it to the baking sheet, gently nudging it off the skewer onto the baking sheet.

Repeat with the remaining banana slices. You may need to rewarm the chocolate once or twice while dipping. If you do, just make sure to add a wee bit of coconut oil to ensure the thin chocolate consistency desired.

Freeze the banana bites until the chocolate is completely solidified, which takes 4–5 hours, or leave them to dry overnight.

## GRAPE POPPERS

Plump grapes speared, dipped in melted Hershey's White Baking Chips, and then rolled in chopped macadamia nuts! Delicious and perfect for any party!

### Ingredients:

**48 FRESH GRAPES**

**1 (12-OZ.) BAG OF HERSHEY'S PREMIER WHITE BAKING CHIPS, OR YOU MAY ALSO USE GHIRARDELLI CHOCOLATE CLASSIC WHITE BAKING CHIPS (11 OZ.)**

**9 OZ. MAUNA LOA MACADAMIAS, DRY ROASTED, UNSALTED**

**SKEWERS**

### Directions:

Wash grapes and dry completely.

Spear each grape with a skewer.

Melt Vanilla Hershey's Premier White Baking Chips in a Wilton® candy melter.

Holding the end of the skewer, dip each grape in the melted Hershey's White Baking Chips; allow excess coating to drip off.

Immediately dip the end of the grape in the chopped nuts and place on wax paper to dry.

## GRILLED CHEESE ON A STICK

This is such fun new way to serve your kids grilled cheese—and it is perfect for dunking!

### Ingredients:

**12 SLICES SANDWICH BREAD**

**6 SLICES KRAFT AMERICAN SINGLES SHARP CHEDDAR CHEESE**

**6 SLICES KRAFT AMERICAN SINGLES WHITE AMERICAN CHEESE**

**2 TBSP. BUTTER**

**1 CAN PROGRESSO™ TOMATO SOUP**

**12 BAMBOO SKEWERS**

### Directions:

Lay out pieces of sandwich bread on a cutting board. Use a rolling pin to flatten. Then use a knife to cut the crusts off of each piece of flattened bread.

Place half a slice of cheddar and half a slice of American cheese on top of each slice of bread, then roll up tightly to form a grilled cheese roll.

Meanwhile, heat butter in a skillet over medium heat until melted. Place the grilled cheese rolls (about 3 at a time) seam-side down in the skillet, and cook on all sides until the bread is toasted and the cheese is melted. You can press the rolls down with a spatula to be sure that they do not unfold while cooking.

Spear each roll with a bamboo skewer and place on serving platter

Remove and repeat with the remaining sandwiches, adding more melted butter if necessary.

Serve immediately with tomato soup as a dipping sauce.

# ZUCCHINI ROLLS

*Ingredients:*

**2 LBS. ZUCCHINI (2–3 LARGE ZUCCHINIS)**

**¼ CUP EXTRA VIRGIN OLIVE OIL**

**A PINCH OF SALT AND PEPPER**

**½ CUP PARMIGIANO–REGGIANO, GRATED**

**½ CUP OF ANTHONY'S PESTO SAUCE (SEE ANTHONY'S SPAGHETTI & MEATBALL STICK)**

*Directions:*

Cut the stems off the zucchinis, then slice them longways into long, thin ribbons. They should be about ⅛-inch thick. If they're too thin, they won't stand up on the own, but if they're too thick, they won't be flexible enough to roll. Brush each one with a little olive oil and sprinkle both sides with salt and pepper.

Heat the grill to high, and do a quick sear of the zucchini. Since they are really thin, they should only be on the grill for less than a minute—just enough to take the raw edge off and so that they have little grill marks when they are finished. Remove the grilled zucchini ribbons and place them on a plate.

In a food processor, mix Anthony's Pesto Sauce with equal parts of Parmigiano cheese, or you can use your favorite goat cheese. Spread the pesto cheese mix on the zucchini ribbon and then roll. Spear the roll with a skewer and place on serving platter.

**PARTY FOODS IN A JAR**

Food in a jar is a special way to style your food and treats. It makes almost any meal-on-the-go perfectly portable for parties on location, like at a bouncy house venue or an indoor racetrack, and it's a creative option if you're looking to forgo the usual pizza party. You can create a party to remember with a visually pleasing menu of jarred meal creations. So it's time to get your creative cap on and start whipping up something new in your very own kitchen. Mason jars have become a big part of party styling lately because of how cute they look in a table setting and how versatile they can be in displaying all kinds of party foods. The jars are great for their looks as well as their functionality. Mason jars are airtight, dishwasher safe, easy to clean, microwave safe (without the lid), and resilient. I recommend getting your jars at Walmart because they have an off-brand that is a great deal and they can be used again and again. For even more amazing jarred food options you can join me on "Mason Jar Mondays" on my blog at www.ILovePartyStyle.com.

## BREAKFAST IN A JAR

Are the kids in a rush in the morning? Do you have a house full of slumber party guests? What better way to serve a quick and easy breakfast than a Breakfast in a Jar?

Layer scrambled eggs, crispy hash browns, and cheddar cheese in a jar and top with crispy bacon or sausage pieces. Top it off with a sprig of cilantro.

You can even prep this one the night before. Line the jars up on a cookie sheet and throw it in the oven for 10 minutes.

## CUPCAKE IN A JAR

Making a cupcake in a jar is surprisingly easy. You just bake your favorite cake recipe as cupcakes using basic cupcake liners in a regular muffin pan. When your cupcakes are fully cooled and ready to find their new home in a jar, cut each one horizontally in half. Place one half in the bottom of the jar. This next part will make your treat super cute or a disaster: pipe your frosting in—do not spoon it into the jar! Pipe frosting around cupcake, add another cake piece, and pipe more frosting—and so on, until you reach the top of your jar top with one last swirl of frosting and sprinkles. Sometimes, I like to do it up by adding chocolate chips, peanut butter, or fruit in between the layers. Don't be afraid to have fun and be creative.

## VEGGIE SNACK JAR

The kids and adults at your party can dip-and-go while they enjoy a no-guilt, healthy snack.

*Ingredients:*

**2 TO 3 TBSP. OF A DRESSING OF YOUR CHOICE (I LIKE RANCH OR A GREEK YOGURT DRESSING)**

*Ingredients for Homemade Greek Yogurt Dressing:*

**3 TABLESPOONS PLAIN GREEK YOGURT**

**DRIZZLE OF GARLIC- AND CHILI-INFUSED OLIVE OIL**

**1 TEASPOON DRIED DILL**

**½ TEASPOON DRIED PARSLEY**

**SEA SALT AND CRACKED PEPPER, TO TASTE**

**10 TO 12 SLICES OF CUCUMBER, CARROTS, AND CELERY CUT LONGWISE**

*Directions:*

If making homemade Greek yogurt dressing, mix all ingredients well, adjusting spices as necessary to achieve desired flavor.

Place dressing of choice at the bottom of a mason jar.

Cut vegetables to fit in the jar and place them inside.

## TACO SALAD IN A JAR

When you're looking for a Mexican food experience for your kid's party, what could be more fun than a taco salad in a jar served with corn chips and limeade? It's the perfect, no-mess fiesta meal.

*Ingredients:*

¼ CUP BLACK BEANS

¼ CUP KERNEL CORN (I LOVE THE FROZEN GRILLED CORN FROM TRADER JOE'S)

8 CHERRY TOMATOES

½ CUP FRESH SHREDDED ROMAINE

8 TORTILLA CHIP STRIPS

1 OZ. GRATED CHEDDAR CHEESE

2 TBSP. OF YOUR FAVORITE SALSA

*Directions:*

Start layering in the ingredients. When you are ready to eat it, give it a good shake to mix the ingredients and it's ready to go. Fun mason jar labels for this recipe are available on www.ILovePartyStyle.com for FREE download.

# LASAGNA PASTA IN A JAR

## Ingredients:

**TOMATO SAUCE**

**HOMEMADE PASTA SHEETS**

**MOZZARELLA CHEESE**

**SHREDDED CHEESE**

**RICOTTA CHEESE**

## Directions:

Start with your favorite meat sauce and store-bought lasagna noodles. After you cook the lasagna noodles, carefully roll them out. Once your pasta is rolled out, use the rim of the jar (I use 16-oz. wide-mouth pint jars) as a cutter to make your pasta layer rounds. As you build the lasagna, it will be tough to get the rounds into the bottom of the jars and they will not be flat. It doesn't have to be perfect!

As you move up in the jar, it will get easier. Add sauce between the layers, then at about a fourth of the way up the jar, add lots of mozzarella cheese. Then for the top half, use the tomato sauce with mozzarella and ricotta. At the top, add some extra mozzarella cheese to glue the top layers together. Be careful not to bake at a temperature that is too hot. Bake at 315–325° for 45 minutes.

Allow the jars to cool for at least 15 minutes before handling.

It takes three rounds to fill a 6-oz. jar. If you make a regular batch of pasta, it will fill 6 jars from top to bottom or, in this case, bottom to top.

## MASHED POTATO & POPCORN CHICKEN MEAL IN A JAR

This one is fun and each can be heated in the oven or microwave (without the lid). This jar of home-cooked goodness makes for a quick, fun, and easy-to-serve BBQ dinner to serve the kids on the patio after a busy summer day.

*Ingredients:*

*Directions:*

**MASHED POTATOES (YOU CAN USE INSTANT OR MAKE THEM FROM SCRATCH)**

**GRILLED CORN (I USE CORN FROM THE FROZEN FOOD SECTION OF TRADER JOE'S)**

**4 PIECES OF POPCORN CHICKEN, BBQ CHICKEN, OR ANY KIND OF CHICKEN PIECES**

**¼ CUP OF SHREDDED CHEDDAR CHEESE**

**BROWN GRAVY**

Layer ingredients in a medium mason jar and heat in the oven or microwave.

# PIE IN A JAR

## Ingredients:

**8 (½-PINT) OVEN-SAFE GLASS JARS**

**YOUR FAVORITE 2 (9-INCH) PIE CRUST RECIPE**

**4 CUPS PIE FILLING, (½-CUP FILLING PER PIE)**

**4 TBSP. COLD UNSALTED BUTTER, CUBED**

**MELTED BUTTER, FOR TOPPING**

**HONEY, FOR TOPPING**

**SUGAR, FOR TOPPING**

## Directions:

Make your favorite pie crust recipe. Store-bought pie dough will also work in a pinch.

Roll out the dough on a floured surface. Using the rim of the jar as a cutter, gently cut 8 circles from the dough. The circles will be the tops of your pies. Line each oven-safe mason jar with the remaining dough. Working the dough as little as possible, make sure that the dough is pressed tightly against the entire surface area of the jar up to about half an inch from the top.

Once each jar is lined with pie dough, fill with ½ cup of your preferred pie filling.

Normally a recipe for pie filling for 1 (9-inch) pie, will make 8 Pies in a Jar. Place ½ tablespoon of butter on top of each pie.

Top each jar with the pie dough circles, or create an old-fashioned lattice pattern or a crumb topping to the pie. Make sure you put a vent in the top of the crust by knifing a small slit so that steam can escape. Using your fingers, or a fork, pinch and crease the pieces of dough together.

Brush each pie crust with melted butter and honey or sprinkle with sugar.

Preheat the oven to 400°F. Bake 40–45 minutes, or until the crust is golden brown and the filling is bubbly.

# S'MORES IN A JAR

## Ingredients:

**1½ CUPS COLD MILK**

**2 BOXES (3.2-OZ. EACH) JELL-O MOUSSE, CHOCOLATE FLAVOR**

**1 CUP JET-PUFFED MINIATURE MARSHMALLOWS**

**1 (8-OZ.) CONTAINER COOL WHIP**

**1 (24-OZ.) BOTTLE HERSHEY'S CHOCOLATE SYRUP**

**15 SHEETS HONEY MAID HONEY GRAHAM CRACKERS, CRUSHED**

**1 BAG HERSHEY'S MILK CHOCOLATE BAKING CHIPS 11.5 OZ**

**1 CUP JET-PUFFED MALLOW BITS**

**1 SHEET HONEY MAID HONEY GRAHAM CRACKERS, SET ASIDE FOR GARNISH**

## Directions:

In a large mixing bowl, combine milk and Jell-O Mousse mix. Mix on low speed for 30 seconds, then on medium speed for four minutes. Once finished mixing, set in refrigerator until ready to use.

In a microwave-safe bowl, add miniature marshmallows and Cool Whip; microwave for 30 seconds. Then, remove the bowl from microwave and stir well, mixing both the marshmallows and whipped cream together. Then, add in the remaining Cool Whip and mix.

To top the jars in chocolate and Graham cracker crumbs, pour 6 tablespoons Hershey's Chocolate Syrup into a plate and dip the opening of your jar into the chocolate syrup, then into the crushed graham cracker mixture. Repeat with each of the remaining jars.

Next, fill your jars by spooning approximately 4 tablespoons of graham cracker crumbs into the bottom of each jar.

Now spoon a layer of your Cool Whip and Jet-Puffed Miniature Marshmallow mixture into each jar, using approximately ½ cup for each jar. Add a layer of chocolate chips. Then spoon your mousse mixture into each jar, using ½–⅔ cup of mousse, and then add another layer of chocolate chips.

Sprinkle the additional graham cracker crumbs on top of mousse layer, followed by an additional scoop of Cool Whip and marshmallow mixture. Sprinkle Jet-

Puffed Mallow Bits on top and add a ¼-sheet of graham crackers to the top for garnish (if desired, dip the Graham cracker into the mousse and sprinkle with Mallow Bits).

Chill in refrigerator until ready to serve.

# MAC & CHEESE JAR

## Ingredients:

½ LB. ELBOW MACARONI

2¼ CUPS MILK

6 TBSP. UNSALTED BUTTER

¼ CUP ALL-PURPOSE FLOUR

2½ CUP SHREDDED SHARP CHEDDAR CHEESE

½ CUP GRATED MOZZARELLA CHEESE

½ TEASPOON SALT

⅓ CUP GRATED PARMESAN CHEESE

¾ CUP FRESH BREADCRUMBS

6 (8-OZ.) CANNING JARS

## Directions:

Preheat oven to 375°. Cook the macaroni in a large pot of boiling salt water for 6 minutes until al dente. Drain macaroni, run cold water over it to stop the cooking, and set aside in a large bowl.

Heat milk until warm, but do not scorch milk. Melt 4 tablespoons of butter in a medium saucepan over medium heat. Stir in flour and mix constantly for 2 minutes until blended, bubbling, and is smooth and pasty. Gradually whisk in the warm milk and cook for 5 minutes, stirring constantly with a whisk until the mixture becomes smooth and thickens. Remove the sauce from the heat and add salt, mixing until incorporated. Gradually mix in the mozzarella cheese and cheddar cheese until blended, stirring until smooth. Add cheese mixture to the macaroni and mix until well coated. Fill the jars with the macaroni and cheese mixture.

Melt the remaining butter. Toss the Parmesan cheese, breadcrumbs, and butter together and sprinkle on top of macaroni and cheese until covered.

Place in jars in the middle of the oven and bake for 15 – 20 minutes.

Watch for over-browning toward the end of the baking time. The cheese sauce may bubble over, so you may want to place the jars on a rack on a baking sheet. If you're eating the macaroni and cheese right away, go ahead and fill 6 jars to the top. If you are planning to save it for later, use more jars (7 to 8) leaving room for the lids. You can use any kind of cheese you desire—it's all a matter of taste. You can add other ingredients such as bacon or bits of ham or sausage.

If you wish to make this macaroni and cheese recipe in a casserole dish instead of the 6 jars, follow the same directions. Fill a 1½-quart casserole dish with all of the macaroni and cheese mixture, baking the casserole for 25 to 30 minutes.

Kids love these macaroni and cheese jars. This recipe is easy enough for the kids to add a helping hand. They make excellent leftovers or for lunch the next day. We make extras for that very reason. Enjoy.

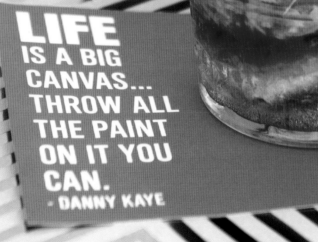

LIFE
IS A BIG
CANVAS...
THROW ALL
THE PAINT
ON IT YOU
CAN.
- DANNY KAYE

## PIZZA IN A JAR

Pizza in a jar is a hit with the kids because they love pizza and putting it into a jar is just a fun new way to serve it. The serving size for these jars is for the teenager and above crowd. Here's what you are going to need to create your own your pizza in a jar:

*Ingredients:*

**ENGLISH MUFFINS**

**TOMATO SAUCE**

**MOZZARELLA CHEESE**

**MASON JARS**

**MINI PEPPERONIS**

**OPTIONAL: TOPPINGS, SUCH AS FRUIT OR VEGETABLES**

*Directions:*

Start with one layer English muffin. Use the lid of the jar to cut out the perfect round shape. Then add sauce and cheese. Next, add half of your English muffin, more sauce and cheese, and top with little mini pepperonis Bake it at 375°F for 15–20 minutes, or until it is beginning to crisp and brown. Serve immediately.

## FRUIT DRINK JAR

Fruit-infused water is the go-to drink for any summer get-together. It can be fruit or veggie flavored. They are simple to make, and with the several options to infuse in the water, you could keep coming up with new mixed fruit and veggie combinations party after party. Citrus with cucumber, berries such as blueberry or raspberry combined with mint, and lemon with lavender are some of my favorite infused water combinations.

*Ingredients:*

**FRESH FRUIT, VEGETABLES, AND HERBS**

**WATER**

**MASON JARS**

**STRAWS**

### FRUITS AND VEGETABLES TO USE

The fresher the fruit, the better the taste; so if you have a farmer's market nearby, then you should visit there first to score the freshest flavors for your drinks. You can choose any fruit or veggie your child likes to infuse your water with, but here are a few of the favorites from recent parties.

| | | |
|---|---|---|
| orange | grapefruit | blueberries |
| lemon | cucumber | strawberries |
| lime | mint | blackberries |

*Directions:*

*Citrus-Infused Water*

Slice the orange, grapefruit, lemon, and lime into slices. Add the slices to a mason jar and fill to the top with fresh, filtered water. Securely screw on the lid and store in the refrigerator until ready to drink.

*Berry-Infused Water*

Add the fresh, rinsed berries to a mason jar. Fill to the top with fresh, filtered water and securely screw on the lid. Store in the refrigerator until ready to drink.

*Cucumber-Mint-Infused Water*

Slice the cucumber into slices and rinse the mint leaves. Add the cucumber slices and mint leaves to a mason jar and fill to the top with fresh, filtered water. Securely screw on the lid and store in the refrigerator until ready to drink.

Tip: For last-minute drinks, add frozen fruit chunks to water. These are great for impromptu guests or if you forget to make a fresh batch of fruit-infused water.

# CANDY
## *calculations*

Creating the perfect candy spread can be tricky. Too much or too little and you'll be scrambling to re-organize your treat display.

***To fill a half-gallon jar,*** use this fool-proof guide for measuring the perfect amount of candy.

| SIXLETS | GUM BALLS | CHOCOLATE ALMONDS | TAFFY |
|---|---|---|---|
|  |  |  |  |
| 3 POUNDS | 2¹/² POUNDS | 3 POUNDS | 1¹/² POUNDS |

### *And More!*
Wrapped candy ..... 1¹/² pounds
Malt balls ..... 2¹/² pounds
M&M's ..... 3 pounds
Licorice pastels ..... 4 pounds
Jelly beans ..... 4 pounds

I am a huge fan of interactive food stations for kid's parties. Unique food stations are trending and will be the "must have" thing for your next children's birthday party. Plan a variety of stations covering anything from breakfast to dessert. There is sure to be a station perfect for your party and your style. I've created ten delicious food bars and stations that are easy to create and that will have your guests talking and your kids enjoying their special day. I have created food labels, signage, banners, and thank-you tags for each of these themes that you can use and customize for your special occasion. They are available for free download in the book section of the Gemma's Party Style Blog.

## PANCAKE STATION

A pancake breakfast is perfect for a sleepover or a weekend treat. You will want to start with fresh buttermilk silver dollar pancakes. I always opt for a Bisquick Shake-and-Pour to make the pancakes. Mini pancakes are best for styling a station like this because the minis make for the perfect little sandwich or to stack up on a flag skewer for an adorable display. Kids can top and stack and fill their pancakes however they like. Along with the pancakes for this station, I serve Nutella, several types of syrup, whipped cream, and butter. I also choose to serve fresh fruit, like my favorite red raspberries, blueberries, black raspberries, strawberries, and bananas. The options are endless; customize with toppings that you or your child love to have on a pancake and you can't go wrong. We thought a great way to really make this display pop was to serve milk shots with sprinkles-rimmed shot glasses. I always use Fairlife whole milk.

## DOUGHNUT STATION

This fun sleepover station was part of a home party celebrating a twelfth birthday. Hannah loves everything vintage, so we carved out this station with dunk-and-drink doughnut holes floating over vintage glasses from her great-grandmother's Singing Hills Golf Club glass set. We also had doughnut bags served up on an old hand-carved table. An underwood typewriter added to the look. We couldn't go all vintage, so we had the amazing doughnuts sign made and glittered by "ten 23 designs," announcing the world's best doughnuts, which were being served up by Sidecar Doughnuts & Coffee located in Costa Mesa, CA, which is right around the corner from us. It is a popular spot because they serve up doughnuts in some amazing flavors like the ones that we have in this party including:

• Samoa: a pineapple coconut cake doughnut topped with chocolate, caramel, and toasted coconut.

• Cardamom Orange: an orange and cardamom cake doughnut topped with house-made cardamom streusel.

• Strawberry Buttermilk Huckleberry: an Oregon huckleberry cake doughnut with huckleberry glaze.

• Peanut Butter, Banana, and Chocolate: a doughnut raised and topped with peanut butter mousse, Callebaut Chocolate glaze, and slices of fresh banana.

• Hibiscus: raised and topped with Hibiscus "Jamaica" glaze.

• Passion Fruit Meringue: raised and topped with passion fruit glaze, passion fruit curd, and finished with toasted homemade meringue.

• The guys loved the Maple Bacon raised doughnut topped with pure Vermont maple syrup glaze and crisp Niman Ranch bacon. Yum!

• The Rosemary: a rosemary-infused doughnut topped with homemade rosemary glaze and a fresh rosemary blossom.

And there were many, many more—you can easily make a doughnut station happen for your party.

## POPCORN STATION

The popcorn station came to be as I wanted to do something special for a "movie classics" themed party.

I had planned a popcorn wagon, but train was forecasted for the party date and the full-sized theme-park-styled popcorn wagon would not fit in the house, so I needed to change things up—and a popcorn station was the perfect answer!

I got a vintage store counter as the station focal point, along with some large, old candy jars to put different types of popcorn in. Through the glass, my guests could see the orange color of the cheese popcorn and the shiny brown coating on the caramel corn. This added excitement for the kids as they came up to pick out their popcorn and fill their popcorn bags. I set up the popcorn station to be interactive so that everyone but the littlest of kids could customize their own bags of popcorn. The food prep was really simple since I bought bags of fresh pre-popped popcorn I ordered from a popcorn-only store at the mall by my house.

I also picked up some vintage-styled salt shakers from the local restaurant supply store and put custom printable labels on them. I put Pink Himalayan salt in one, coarse sea salt in another, Lawry's Season salt in another, and garlic salt in another. I also put other flavors in the shakers like cheddar cheese and nacho cheese popcorn seasoning that I ordered online from www.KernelSeasons.com. Additional candies, sprinkles, toffee, candied nuts, and peanuts were offered for those wanting a sweet and salty mix. The kids loved the candy and nut mixes almost as much as I did.

I purposely picked out plain old buttered popcorn, plus five very unusual popcorn flavors from a popcorn store at the mall so that I would have familiar popcorn, but also some exciting, unique choices for the guests. My son created a simple game called "Name that Popcorn Flavor" and his best buddy was the only person to guess all six of the popcorn flavors and was crowned the winner.

## GRILLED CHEESE STATION

I put my own twist on classic grilled cheese. A grilled cheese station is one of the latest party and wedding station trends, as it is popular with guests of all ages. My grilled cheese station was beautifully presented, fresh, fun, and delicious. We had toasters, George Foreman grills, and a panini press so that the guests could build a personalized grilled cheese or even a mini panini on their choice of breads. We had more than just good old-fashioned Kraft American Cheeses Slices; we included mozzarella cheese for the stringy fun and we raided Trader Joe's for everything from Romano to blueberry goat cheese. Next to the cheese selection, there were small, shot-sized glasses filled with a very delicious tomato bisque. This made for the ultimate comfort food for my kids and was a huge success.

This station is also wonderful when paired with a soup station. The taste is classic good and makes for an easy lunchtime meal for the party guests.

## TRAIL MIX STATION

A trail mix bar is definitely a popular party trend nowadays. They are really big for the casual, rustic-themed parties in the summer or fall. This station fits in real well for themed parties such as lumberjack, hiking, fishing, summer camp, and more. Not only is it great having guests gather around and choose their treats, but it is also great as a host to simply set out your favorite nuts, white raisins, red raisins, Ocean Spray Craisins, oats, dried fruits and berries, and maybe even some candies and marshmallows. Consider having vintage-style tea tins and bread boxes. Just add little labels on sticks to help guests make their choices! Offer an eye-catching array of ingredients to "mix"! Consider items that are sweet, savory, and salty. Some examples include: chocolate chips, M&M's, walnuts, pistachios, cashews, peanuts, and almonds, sunflower seeds, mini marshmallows, and pretzels. You can also opt for some spicy choices that are flavored with hot sauce, cajun, wasabi, and hot or sweet BBQ sauce. You can also include dried vegetables like carrot chips or dried jicama chips. Since your theme and venue are most likely to be alpine and rustic looking, make use of woodsy elements like wood chips, pine-log-looking branches, and woven country baskets. Other options would be wood slabs, twigs, berries, bunches of wheat, acorns, pine cones, and colorful wildflowers.

The best part about this station is that trail mix is filling, but absolutely no cooking or baking is required!

## NACHO STATION

This nacho station is easy to plan, stock, and set up. It is convenient for guest of all ages to create their own nachos, and most people are familiar with it nowadays. People, especially kids, seem to really get excited about making their own nachos. This station is a great idea for any party. My kids created a nacho bar for my niece's birthday, and it became the gathering point for the guests! The teenagers loved the nacho bar as much I do.

If you are going to be hosting a large party, it may be easier to keep it stocked with canned nacho cheese; warehouse stores sell giant cans of nacho cheese! For this station I added lot of toppings, like jalapeños, bell peppers, sour cream, hot salsa, mild salsa, green salsa, mango salsa, pineapple salsa, chopped tomato, chopped cilantro, chopped pineapple, chopped roasted garlic, chopped cheeses, Tabasco sauce, Tapatio Hot Sauce, Red Hots sauce, Sriracha sauce, pinto beans, black beans, green onions, tomatoes, and guacamole. I also like to include ground beef flavored with a taco seasoning and freshly BBQ'd and shredded chicken, pork, and beef. You can customize your station with any toppings that you choose, but this is what I usually start with when I serve nachos. I also like to use the white paper nacho trays, which you can get at a restaurant supply store or Costco.

## CANDY STATION

Candy stations are popping up at all types of parties—from weddings and bridal showers to birthdays and baby showers. Choose your candies wisely. The hard, shiny candies can get pricey. Think about the venue of your party as you plan out your candy station. Will the day be hot or humid? Consider buying individually wrapped candies and chocolates that won't stick together, or opt for hard candies that won't melt, instead of soft caramels or chocolates. Candies can be had in a variety of colors so find some that match your theme to create a visual highlight. Design your candy station accordingly with varieties in color and candy sizes on display in glass jars. Present the candy like they are your trophies; create height in your display for delicious drama! Target has an excellent selection of colored hard candies just for parties.

To make multiple tiers on the table, use risers under the tablecloth or use wooden crates. Glass or other transparent containers are the best for showing it off and making and a dazzling display. Giant jars and goblets look stunning, but consider that you will need to fill those extra-large containers with a lot of candy, so plan accordingly. Try to assemble a wide variety of different shapes and types of containers for the best visual appeal. Thrift stores and discount stores like Marshalls and TJ Maxx can be excellent sources for inexpensive bowls, jars, and vases. Mix and match giant margarita glasses, vintage dime-store candy jars, flared bowls, and trifle containers with champagne flutes, or mini bowls, popcorn boxes, and pretty little organza bags.

As you load the candy, remember that labels are a must! Not only do they look cute, but they help your guests navigate the station and choose candies that they like. Supply candy bags for the kids to load up with their favorite treats. I like to use small plain white bags, known as "2-pound" size. You can get them at Smart & Final, Costco, and you can also find them online. You can also use "merchandise bags," which are flat paper bags. With the smaller bags you can run them through your printer, so you can easily and cheaply customize them at home. Keep in mind that the bigger the bag, the more candy guests are likely to take. I customized my bags with labels that I designed and printed out on full-page label sheets. Then all I had to do was cut them to stick them on bag!

## SNOW CONE STATION

Snow cones are a great treat for a party on a warm day. The syrups are usually colored and having a variety of flavors or colors will be the thing that makes this exciting for the kids. Snow Cone syrup is a little pricey, but you can make your own homemade syrup.

You will need just a few things to make your own homemade snow cone syrup:

> 1 cup white granulated sugar

> 1 cup water

> Crushed ice

1 (.22-oz.) packet Kool-Aid drink mix (store brand drink mixes are usually smaller (.15-oz.) but will work too)

I recommend heating your water in the microwave instead of on the stovetop. If you let it boil with the sugar in it, it will thicken.

Once your water is boiling (about 3 minutes), remove it (carefully!) and add sugar. Whisk until dissolved. Then add in 1 packet of Kool-Aid (or other drink mix). Whisk until dissolved. Allow to cool fully. It's easy to pour into the bottles when cool.

Serve over crushed ice. Store the leftover syrup in refrigerator.

As for the bottles, you'll need "bottled water" bottles with squeeze tops. You can label them with the different flavors with printables or with scrapbook paper.

## LEMONADE STATION

If you are thinking about planning a party, and are concerned about the standard soft drink options being boring, look no further than lemonade. Try a stab at your own beautiful modern interpretation of the "Lemonade Stand." Think old-school lemonade stand meets fun, fabulous mix-ins to create a new spin on that old summer standard. Lemonade is a great drink for summer parties. Whether you make it fresh, buy it at the store, or use a powdered mix, it's hard to go wrong with cold lemonade on a hot day. Here are some of my fun ideas to dress up your lemonade. Start with large containers or pitchers of lemonade. Add bowls of your favorite flavors: think spices, fruit, herbs, liquor, or even Kool-Aid mixes for the kids. Be creative. Almost anything tastes good with lemonade as the base!

# MILK SHAKE STATION

This last party station is one after my own heart. Who wouldn't want to have a milk shake at a birthday party? Refreshingly cold, creamy, and delicious . . . it is a warm day as I write this section and now I think I want a milk shake, like right now!

My family knows all too well that ice cream is my all-time favorite treat. Although some would think that cake is my favorite, it's definitely ice cream. Big kids and little kids agree—we all scream for ice cream! So when I had a chance to use this vintage Retro Milk Shake Party, I was instantly in love with the idea. This station can be set up with a stunning party layout, and it is perfect for a summer family get-together or a child's birthday party.

The setting is an old soda shop with thick milk shake glasses and colored paper straws. From the chalkboard menus to the stand mixers, toppings and vintage straws, this milkshake station has it all. I like the old red, white and chrome color theme of those old soda shops. It makes me smile and crave a bowl of Neapolitan ice cream.

Get a variety of ice cream flavors and pre-scoop them for ease. Arrange them by type on a wax paper or parchment-lined cookie sheet and freeze until very firm. It would be a nice touch if you can find out your guests' favorite ice cream flavors ahead of time. Accommodate dietary restrictions by having a separate tray for special ice creams (such as vegan, nut-free, lactose-free) to avoid any issues. When you're ready to party, place the tray on another tray that is filled with ice sprinkled with salt. This helps lower the freezing temperature of water which makes the ice stay frozen longer.

Pour your milk into a glass jar or pitcher with a lid and set them in a bucket or bowl of ice to keep cold. You can even put out a variety of flavored syrups like chocolate, coconut, or strawberry, so the kids can create their very own secret milkshake concoction! Provide a variety of dessert add-ins like brownies, cookies, and cake; or candies like chocolate, butterscotch, caramel, malted milk balls, Snickers, M&M's, and Butterfinger bar. Most of all, include fruits like strawberries, blueberries, raspberries, peaches, bananas, or pineapple chunks. Lastly, top with marshmallow creme, and whipped cream.

Be sure to include the vintage soda shop decorations to get the full scoop (no pun intended) on this popular party station.

**PARTY STYLE CELEBRATIONS**

*chapter ten*

I really love what I do for a living since styling parties is such a great creative outlet, but I also love to see how excited my clients get when they see the party that was designed for them. In the following pages I share some examples of parties that I think showcase what you can do with just a little bit of planning. These are parties that include a variety of elements that I cover in this book, and all are displayed to provide you with inspiration and direction as you work on creating a party for your guest of honor. Most of the parties I style include pieces and design elements that I have custom-ordered from extraordinarily talented people. I am very lucky to work with the worlds most amazing style makers.  I have also had the opportunity to work with some wonderfully creative party stylists over the past few years with *Party Style Magazine*, and some of these talents are so exceptional that I felt compelled to include them in this book and share their eye for design and use of color. I can't wait for you to turn the page and get inspired.

Cowgirl Chic

Create a special place for the mom-to-be to sit, and wow the guests with hanging cupcake stands. Small, thoughtful details create lifelong memories.

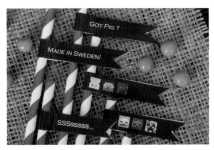

Egg Hunt

Use unique décor and bright colors. Don't be afraid to step out of your normal routine on the holidays—it's about having fun with your style. Here we peeped out a simple grocery store cake.

frosted gumballs

**COOL COLORS AND UNIQUE PATTERNS CAN CREATE A THEME ON THEIR OWN.**

Spring Fling

Tea Party

The "Afternoon Tea" was a time that the family gathered the kids together after school to have a small meal that would carry them over until dinner. This Birthday Tea for twin girls is full of classic ideas and modern enjoyments, including a light teatime menu, a sweetheart table for the birthday girls, paper china plates perfect for kids, and fun wooden utensils.

# Camp Party —

Happy Birthday
## CAMP HANNAH
*The Great Outdoors*

2015

MAKE YOUR OWN PATH

JOIN US IN THE FOREST

*Hannah Grace*

- IS TURNING -

*Eight*

>>> RSVP: GEMMA 949. 555. 1234 <<<
CAMPHANNAH@GMAIL. COM
#CAMPHANNAH

Happy Birthday
CAMP HANNAH
*The Great Outdoors*

Camping is a great backyard or park party idea. You can create classic s'mores and play outdoor games, or you can go with a tribal theme or glamping party for girls. The outdoor setting leaves a lot of room for your imagination and style to take the stage.

OWL LOVE YOU FOREVER —

A simple party with sweet treats and easy games, the Owl Always Love You theme is unique and fresh!

# JOKER PARTY

# CREATE A PARTY AROUND WHAT YOUR KIDS LOVE!

Prima Ballerina

Create an out-of-the-box piggy ballerina party with monogramed cookies, costumes made from tulle and décor, a photo station with fun props, and everything glittered in magical gold, even the treats! It's easy to plan a one-of-a-kind dreamland for your ballerina.

**SWEET TREATS, ROMANTIC DRESSES, AND HOLIDAY DECORATIONS MAKE THIS BUNNY PARTY COME TO LIFE.**

# Sweet Bunny Love

FLY AWAY WITH ME, PLANE PARTY

With a classic airplane party in patriotic colors, your little guest of honor's dreams are sure to take flight. Creative cupcake toppers and suitcase cookies create the perfect treat. Line trays of sixlets or colored paper for an added touch.

**FLY AWAY WITH ME! UP INTO THE BLUE SKY, UP INTO THE FLUFFY CLOUDS**

Departures

SUPER HERO

Skate Party

Matching socks create sisterly fun for all the kids. Have each guest pick a pair.
With bright colors and fast wheels, the kids will have so much fun that they'll be rolling in the aisles.

# DRESS UP OZ PARTY —

DRESS UP PARTIES ARE ALWAYS FUN FOR EVERYONE.
COME IN COSTUME OR PICK ONE WHEN YOU ARRIVE.

# RAINBOW PARTY

This theme can be a classic rainbow, a unicorn party, an art party, oranything you can think of that makes a rainbow. The options are limitless with dry pastels & bright rainbows.

# Dinosaur Roar

## HAVE A ROARING GOOD TIME!

### GEMMA TOUCHSTONE & I LOVE PARTY STYLE TEAM

When working on events I have an amazing team of helpers and some amazing style makers helping out. Concept, design, printables, sweets, and catering by www.ILovePartyStyle.com. Photography by Jeanette Dianda. www.jeanettediandaphotography.com Cake by Radiant Cake. Sweets by The Sunday Sweet and Kima's Konfections. Rentals by Party Pieces by Perry. Paper goods from Michaels Craft Stores. For a complete list of vendors for party ideas featured in this book, and for more information about vendors and style makers, visit www.ILovePartyStyle.com.

### GENEVIEVE KEITH, SIMPLY SMASHING EVENTS

*Camp Hannah*

Genevieve Keith is the owner of Simply Smashing Events in Southern Oregon. She began her career in floral design and soon her love of crafting and creating beautiful parties led her into event planning and styling. She and her husband have two adorable little girls, who are an endless source of sparkly inspiration for everyday celebrations. Genevieve can be seen monthly on KDRV News Watch 12 in Medford.

*Vendors*

Printable design by Gemma Touchstone, Party Style. Table design, styling, props, and treats by Simply Smashing Events. Photography by Sara Faith Photography at www.sarafaithphotography.com. Piñata and tassel from Prospect Goods at www.prospectgoods.com. Cupcakes and cake pops by Kristi Jensen at Simply Smashing Events. Cookies and s'mores treats by Sara Marier at Simply Smashing Events.

## LAUREN BORQUEZ, CAPES & CROWNS

*Joker Comic Party*

Lauren Borquez is the founder and styling artist of Capes & Crowns. A self-confessed geek and child at heart, Lauren welcomed the opportunity to have a fun, creative outlet when she decided to stay at home to raise her two boys. Kal-El and Logan (both named after superheroes) are the inspiration behind all of her creative energy. Lauren's trademark style is thinking outside the box and using unique themes. Lauren is currently a contributing stylist for *Party Style Magazine* and several other publications. After winning the 2013 Pottery Barn stylist competition, she continued to work with them, as well as several other national brands like Pottery Barn Kids, Shindigz, Happy Family, and many others. She resides in a quaint town in the northern part of Alabama with her husband Chris and her two superheroes.

*Vendors*

Concept and styling by Capes & Crowns at www.facebook.com/capesandcrownsparties. Photography by Danielle McCann Photography at www.facebook.com/dmccannphotography. Hair and makeup by Laren Lindholm. Printables by Whimsically Detailed. Harley Costume by Atutudes Hand Made Tutus. Joker Costume by Rabbit Woods Design. Harley and Joker custom painted pieces by Salty Inspirations Art. Cake and red and black macarons by Gourmet Gal Cakes, Harley and Joker props by CS Cute Crafts, Harley and Joker cupcake pedestals by Storybook Stands. Joker painting by Amanda Brickley-Price. Joker name banner by Girl Bye. Joker table cupcake toppers by Les Pop Sweets. Custom Cookies (Joker and 2 cookies on Harley table) by Bake or Eat Sweets. Harley print design cookies by 5 by Five Designs. Cake topper by Plastic Smith. Mad Love felt table dropper by Linc Kids. Purple tablecloth by Candy Crush Events. Mad Love banner by Beautiful Paper Crafts. Red tablecloth by Sparkle Soirée. Covered Oreos and pudding toppers by Kima's Konfections. Painted letters by Cali Dreamin. Joker and Harley wineglasses by Antoni's Art Asylum. Brownies by Q's Cake, Cupcakes and Sweets. Cake pops by Cupcake Novelties. Topiary by Edible Weddings. Green and purple macarons by Wedding2 Baby. Favor bags by Planning with Jacen. Red and black balloons and green balloon with tassel by Balloon and Paper. Green and purple tassel banner by Simply Nesting.

## MIRANDA THOMPSON, WHIMSICALLY DETAILED

*Piggy Prima Ballerina*

Miranda is the creative mind behind Whimsically Detailed, a creative event–planning firm in Texas. She loves putting together baby showers and birthday parties. Miranda also creates unique event printables. For planning or styling, her firm is located just outside of San Antonio, Texas, in Boerne, or find her products online at www.whimsicallydetailed.com.

Event & styling by Whimsically Detailed. Photos by Pagette Callender Photography. Desserts by MJ Occasions and by Miranda Thompson at Whimsically Detailed.

## Dino Party

Event styling, invitations, dino shirts, and fabric bunting by Whimsically Detailed. Photography by Pagette Callender Photography. Dino Tails by Bone Head Studios. Dino digs, party horns, and palm tree stirrers by Oh Goodie Designs. Berry baskets and Kraft Food liners, straws, bamboo cups, and cones by Cute Kids Food Box. Dino wreaths by The Knock Knock Factory. Mini glitter name buntings by The Purple Pug. Candy apples, volcano pops, macarons, mini chocolate doughnuts, and cakes by MJ Occasions. Brigadeiros by Simply Brigadeiro. Dino cake pops by Maskipops. Lollipops by Vintage Confections. Cookies by Artfully Delicious. Fondant cupcake toppers and fondant-topped Oreos by Love & Sugar Kisses.

## LYNDA CORREA, STORYBOOK BLISS LLC.

## Bunny Love

A self-taught newbie party stylist, Lynda loves sparkly, whimsical, and glamorous things. It's a team effort between Lynda and her husband, who is a chef who graduated from Scottsdale Le Cordon Bleu and really adds to the catering side of our business with his artful and delicious culinary specialties. Together, they specialize in party styling, catering, and customized chocolate-covered shortbread cookies.

## Vendors

Event styling, concept, and gold cookie tower by Storybook Bliss at www.facebook.com/StorybookBliss or on Instagram @storybook_bliss. Photography by Natalie Orona Photography at www.facebook.com/NatOrona or on Instagram @natorona. Bunny Cake and cupcakes by Cleverly Sweet at www.facebook.com/CleverlySweet or on Instagram @cleverlysweet. Bunny and floral sugar cookies by Sugared Hearts Bakery at www.facebook.com/SugaredHeartsBakery or on Instagram @sugaredhearts. Bunny banner and tent cards by Lexi Kay Paperie at www.facebook.com/lexikaypaperie or on Instagram @lexi_kay_paperie. Floral spring dresses, floral crowns, and bunny doilies by Michelle Rodriquez at MichelleRodriguezDesigns@yahoo.com or on Instagram @3fairygodmothers. Silver sequin tutu by Bow Ties and Tutu Boutique at www.bowtiesandtutusboutique.com or on Instagram @bowtiesandtutuboutique. Floral bouquet caramel apples by Roni's Sugar Creations at RoniSugarCreations.com or on Instagram @ronisugarcreations.

## KAREN REED, FOREVER YOUR PRINTS, AND ELIZABETH SPRAGUE, LEMONBERRY MOON

## Airplane Birthday

The woman behind the company, Karen Reed, is a truly dedicated wife, mom, and entrepreneur! Running your own business can be incredibly rewarding, and a challenge at times . . . but what job isn't? "You have to have focus with a side of determination," Karen says, "and for me, I have to remember the golden rule. My golden rule is you have to love what you do, or it is not worth doing." Karen loves to partner with Elizabeth Sprague from Lemonberry Moon. Lemonberry Moon started as strictly a portrait photography business, but grew into party planning.

*Vendors*

Party styling & photography by Lemonberry Moon at www.lemonberrymoon.com. Party printables by Forever Your Prints at www.foreveryourprints.com. Embroidered airplane shirt by Great Stitch at www.etsy.com/shop/GreatStitch. Favor boxes by Cute Kids Foodbox at www.etsy.com/shop/CuteKidsFoodbox. Peanut/pretzel containers by Bakers Party Shop at www.bakerspartyshop.com. Paper pinwheels by www.etsy.com/shop/KristynsKreations517. Earth chocolates by Sweetworks at www.sweetworks.net, Fondant cupcake toppers by Lena's Cakes at www.etsy.com/shop/LenasCakes. Cookies by Katie's Creative Baking at www.etsy.com/shop/katieduran.

## PATTY SMITH, PERFECT SERENDIPITY

*I Am Spider-Man Birthday*

Patty Smith is the owner of Perfect Serendipity. Her love for styling celebrations started originally with the design and planning of her own wedding. She has always had a creative streak and dreamed of self-employment. With the inspiration of her family and an excitement for designing, she launched Perfect Serendipity. She finds inspiration through her children and she tries to see things through their eyes. Patty is always thinking outside the box and loves to dream up unique themes. She loves whimsical, charming and imaginary designs. Find her at www.PSPerfectSerendipity.com or on Instagram @psperfectserendipity.

*Vendors*

Set design assistance by Jodi Fuller of Grey Beginnings at www.jodifullerart.com/greybeginnings, www.JodiFullerArt.com, and www.facebook.com/greybeginnings or on Instagram @greybeginnings. Photography by Alisha Shaw Photography at www.AlishaShaw.com or on Instagram @alishashawphotography. Graphic designs by The Blue Egg Events and Design at www.blueeggevents.com and at www.theblueeggevents.etsy.com. Fashion stylist: TNT Tauna at www.tnt-tauna.com. Hairstylist: Erin Seaich at ErinSeaich@hotmail.com. Black New York City silhouette vinyl wall decal and photography and backdrop of New York City skyline with red and blue designs by Rockabye Prints at www.RockaByePrints.etsy.com. Red and black spider piñata by Double K's Piñatas at www.doublekspinatas.etsy.com. White spandex tablecloth by Your Chair Covers at www.yourchaircovers.com or on Instagram @yourchaircovers. Red spider logo and black bridge silhouettes by Ten23 Designs at www.ten23designs.com or on Instagram @ten23designs. Fondant cake by Kima's Konfections at www.kimakonfections.com. Fondant cupcake toppers by Little Shindigs at www.facebook.com/littleshindigsoregonn. French macarons with hand-painted edible art and glitter design by Call Me Combat Cookie at www.callmecombatcookie.etsy.com or on Instagram @callmecombatcookie. Hand-painted sugar cookies by Baking In Heels at www.bakinginheelscookies.com and www.bakinginheels.etsy.com or on Instagram @bakinginheels. Chocolate-covered Oreos with black city silhouette by Gloria, (G. Pop) on Instagram @G.Pop310. Custom lollipops by Vintage Confections at www.vintageconfections.com or on Instagram @vintageconfections. Custom-designed skyscrapers and city park bench by Wendy's Printable Party at www.wendysprintableparty.etsy.com or on Instagram @wendysprintable.party. Custom "Spider Web" and "The Eye of the Spider" pillow designs by Great Stitch at www.greatstitch.com and www.greatstitch.etsy.com or on Instagram @greatstitch. Canvas, paint, and easel party favors by Crate and Party at www.crateandparty.com or on Instagram @crateandparty. Dress suit jacket, pants, shirt, and fedora by Appaman at www.appaman.com or on Instagram @appaman. Spider-Man cufflinks made from vintage Spider-Man comic books by glamMKE at www.glammke.com. Spider-Man boy's necktie by Fafa Tutu at www.FafaTutu.etsy.com and www.facebook.com/shopfafatutu.

GINA LEE

*Skate Party*

Gina Lee is known throughout Southern California as one of the leading children's and family photographers. Her work has been published in *People Magazine*, *Parents Magazine*, *Child Style Magazine*, *Party Style Magazine*, *Family Fun*, and *Mamalode Magazine*. Her work has also been highlighted on the Oprah Winfrey Show and she has had published two book covers for her work. Based in Redlands, California, Gina lives with her husband and three children. She works on location throughout Southern California and she is available for commercial work throughout the United States.

Vendors

Photography by Gina Lee at www.ginaleephoto.com. Cookies by Jess Cookies at www.jesscookies.com. Cake pops and cake by CC Sweets at www.ccsweets.us. Location information available at www.fiestvillage.com.

DANA GRANT

*Dress Up Oz Party Vendors*

Style and photography by Dana Grant Photography. Dorothy's, Glinda's, and flower girls' dresses, red slippers, green heels, and Converse by Evey Rothstein Clothing at www.eveyclothing.com. Hair and makeup by Melody Rachunok at www.hairbymelody.com. Owen and Levi Rachunok as Munchkins and Lily Bos as flower girl Munchkin. Table décor by Serendipitous Events by Julia at www.serendipitouseventsbyjulia.com. Invitation by Christy Schurle at www.onehandspunday.com. Hot air balloon boutonniere, red sparkle bow tie, and green backdrop by Emilee Hegg at www.tastefultatters.com. Glinda model: Maile Roseland at www.seadottir.blogspot.com. Dorothy and the wizard models, vintage suit, ascot, and vintage rings by Alexandria and Spencer Phillips at www.etsy.com/shop/PhillipsandCoVintage. Toto model, Dorothy's bouquet, and Glinda's vintage crown by Rebecca Stringham at www.rebecca-june.blogspot.com. Cookies by Linzy Kearby of Parchment Cookies. Cake by Cakes and Catering by Karie. Yellow bouquet and flower girl flower by Rose Safran at www.rosesafran.wordpress.com.

**TARGET:** The ultimate go-to store for throwing any party, and they are open late so you can get your last-minute items when you're in a pinch—anything from party streamers and craft supplies to blush and lipstick. I always find myself at Target the night before the party—usually for food items, but then I end up redecorating the bathroom.

**ORIENTAL TRADING COMPANY:** This company offers amazing deals on party prizes, favors, and games. Find out more at www.orientaltrading.com.

**KITCHENAID:** The ultimate in home appliances; if you have a KitchenAid mixer and food processer, you can basically make anything.

**MICHAELS:** The party crafting warehouse. You can create and craft any party backdrop or idea with their new recollection lines and goodies; they also carry an amazing selection of Wilton® baking goods. I am at Michaels at least twice a week.

**EPSON:** I love creating pintables, and without my Epson laser jet color printer I would not have such amazing results. I LOVE Epson!

**PAPER SOURCE:** This is my source for unique papers and card making. See www.papersource.com.

**SHOP SWEET LULU:** This online shop carries all the unique party décor and sweet finds you will need for a unique and on-trend party. See www.shopsweetlulu.com.

**FAIR LIFE MILK:** The ultimate milk! It is amazing for cooking and baking. Its reduced sugar has a longer shelf life and more protein, and the filtering process makes it taste amazing.

**CANDY WAREHOUSE:** The best place for party candy and I love the old-fashioned candy selection. Check out what they have to offer at www.candywarehouse.com.

**WILTON®:** Pastry tips, packaging, Candy Melts®, edible pieces, fondant, decorating tools, baking tools, and packaging—Wilton® makes everything you need for parties and baking.

**RADIANT CAKES:** She makes the best cake pops in the world. My resource for amazing cake pops, and they ship! See www.radiantcakes.com.

**PARTY PIECES BY PERRY:** Amazing vintage rentals for small gatherings of 100 or less. See www.partypiecesbyperry.com .

**ARCHIVE:** My go-to for unique party rentals for gatherings of 100 or more. See www.archiverentals.com.

**SHINODA DESIGN CENTER:** The ultimate décor and design warehouse. This resource is California, but they have every kind of vessel, ribbon, silk flower, and prop.

**POTTERY BARN:** Seasonal serving and party pieces are amazing, and Pottery Barn Kids offers unique items for your party.

**HOME GOODS:** This is my go-to resource for entertaining with cake plates and décor; their kids' section is bursting at the seams and every aisle is made to inspire you.

**RONI'S SUGAR CREATIONS:** Roni's candy apples will wow at any party; she ships, and will create something custom and unique for any party. See more at www.RoniSugarCreations.com.

**CATCH MY PARTY:** My favorite party inspiration resource for kids online. This site is jam-packed with free printables, inspirations, and resources. See more at www.catchmyparty.com.

**LUVULU:** My favorite blog for recipes, inspirations, and everything you love in life. See www.Luvulu.com.

**WILLIAMS-SONOMA:** Cooking utensils, unique entertaining finds, and high quality goods. See www.williams-sonoma.com.

**PARTY CITY:** I get all my balloons filled and purchased from Party City, and sometimes I will pick up a small tank to take home. Their new lines of party décor are impressive. I love the square hard plastic plates for adults' and kids' parties. See www.partycity.com.

**MINTED:** Minted offers an amazing array of printed paper goods and ideas, not only for parties but for home décor as well. See www.minted.com.

**MODIFY INK:** A beautiful source for party printables and wall art that you can customize yourself; I am literally in love with this site. See www.modifyink.com.

**BLOGGER ACADEMY:** My resource for all things blogger and for building and sharing your blog.

**MAYESH FLOWERS:** I order all my flowers from Mayesh; they are beautiful and the selection is neverending. See www.mayesh.com

**TINY PRINTS:** Love this resource for online kids' invitations and home décor with a custom twist.

**CHOBANI GREEK YOGURT:** The best pure Greek yogurt to use in your dips and recipes.

**PHILADELPHIA CREAM CHEESE:** The only cream cheese to use while creating your dips and frostings.

**CHEX™ CEREAL:** The main ingredient in almost every party mix is the Magic Chex Mix. Chex cereal is also great for a gluten-free crunch.

**STRAUSS FAMILY FARM CREAMERY:** The best heavy whipping cream to make homemade whipped cream.

**SIXLETS®:** I love to fill jars and use them as tray liners. I use Sixlets® in almost every party in one way or another.

**M&M'S®:** The all-American candy. We use this in our Chex™ mix and trail mix all the time.

**OCEAN SPRAY:** Dried cranberries, canned cranberries, and juice.

**REPUBLIC OF TEA:** Offers caffeine-free flower teas perfect for kids' drink mixes.

**HAMPTON CREEK JUST MAYO:** My kids love this mayo—it's delicious, non-GMO, pea-made mayo without eggs.

**RITZ CRACKERS:** Classic and part of tons of party food recipes.

**PILLSBURY®:** When you don't have time to make cookie dough from scratch, this tastes homemade.

**BOB'S RED FLOUR MILL:** My favorite brand of baking ingredients.

**JET-PUFFED MARSHMALLOW:** I use this all the time.

**COOL WHIP:** A staple ingredient when it comes to kids' foods.

**TRADER JOE'S:** I always find myself raiding their dried fruits, nuts, and cookies.

**WALKERS:** The best pie crust and desserts I make use Walkers Butter Cookies.

**HERSHEY'S:** I frequently use the baking chips and syrups.

## SWEET NOTES

"*Party Style Magazine* offers such a great array of inspiration to many DIY project ideas and beautifully styled parties."

— Alyssa from Just A Little Sparkle at www.justalittlesparkle.com

"Creative Collaborations loves *Party Style Magazine* for creative party ideas. Gemma seems to always have the latest trends and concepts to throw any party or wedding! I adore her ideas."

— Janelle Evans of Creative Collaborations at www.creativecollaborationsje.com

"We love Gemma! She is a vivacious, generous, talented, smart, and ridiculously creative woman. We are huge fans of her designs and cannot wait to share her amazing book."

— Debbie and Nestor Serrano

"*Party Style Magazine* is such a fun place to get great ideas and see some amazing work done by the most talented people in the party industry. I am always honored to be featured, but even more so I'm always excited to see everyone else's work!!"

— Danielle McCann at www.daniellemccannphotography.com

"*Party Style* has been such an inspirational publication to me. To see an entire publication filled with talented small business owners who rock the event industry is amazing! I am so honored to have had my work featured in several issues of the magazine this past year. *Party Style Magazine* is making waves in the event industry and I am excited to be a part it."

— Lauren Sarnoff Atwater at www.ten23designs.com

"*Party Style Magazine* is a phenomenal resource for all of life's celebrations!! We absolutely love it & continue to be in awe of their eye for beauty, trend setting party ideas, collaboration of talented vendors & contributors, and inspirational content for every reader to be benefit from. We are also so grateful that *Party Style Magazine* was willing to give a new party stylist like myself an opportunity to be featured in their magazine. Since being featured, we have gained increased exposure & have made wonderful connections with amazing party stylists & businesses. On a personal level, Gemma has taken the time to mentor, encourage, empower, and inspire upcoming party stylists to be the best they can be."

– Lynda Correa at www.storybookbliss.com

"*Party Style* is a wonderful resource of current party trends, projects, and styles in the event industry. The unique blend of innovative artists, stylists, and crafters makes everyday occasions easier and obtainable for everyone to achieve! With some of the freshest ideas available in our industry, *Party Style* is the place to go! Events by Kate is a proud supporter and is blessed to be a part of *Party Style*!"

– Kate from EBK at www.eventsbykate.com

"I just love *Party Style*; it's full of entertaining party styling, inspiration, and creativity. A great, delicious read for all looking for party ideas."

– Louisa from The Little Big Company at www.tlbc.com.au

"Every edition of *Party Style* is crammed with inspiration, talented artists, and beautiful parties! Being a part of them as a stylist is an amazing experience. I can't wait to see what eye candy Gemma will keep bringing to the party world."

– Christie Skerski from Flaired Affairs at www.facebook.com/flairedaffairs

"Everything Gemma does turns to gold; she has the Midas touch. Style and execution are beyond amazing—every event, every time."

– Anastasia Backstrand at www.tralalainc.com

## A GRATEFUL HEART

I have to say that completing this book has been a huge accomplishment for me. It is something that I have dreamt of since I was a small child, when I used to create folds of paper stapled together into little hand-sketched books with my name drawn funny on the front and a Crayola-and-pencil drawing of my likeness on the back. Thank you, Cedar Fort, for believing in me and in my brand Party Style enough to publish my book and for fulfilling a young girl's dream, because no matter how old I am, it is still that little girl's dream.

It is with a humble and grateful heart that I thank two very important people. Thank you to my sweet love Anthony Mesaros for staying up with me night after night editing the pages and making sure each one is perfect. My love, I couldn't not have done this without you, and I am blessed to have been given such a supportive force and loving companion in my life. Without your kind heart, so many things would not be possible. And thank you to my mother-in-law, Jeanette Dianda: God could not have provided a better mother and friend in this crazy life; although it is tragedy that bonded us, it is your kind heart that maintains my love for you. The fact that you are one of the most talented photographers on the planet is just an added perk to being your daughter-in-law. Who could have ever guessed in 2008 when we shot that first party that it would circulate the Internet and turn into a magazine, a blog, a product line, and now a book? You have been there every step of the way making me look good. Thank you for always being there to shoot my parties and ideas at all hours of the night and day. You have had to follow my crazy schedule. Without your talent this book could have never happened. I always say a stylist is as only as good as her photographer and I thank God you are mine.

Thank you to my children, Noah and Hannah: You have endured the sleepless nights, the quick dinners while I met deadlines, and the glitter and confetti along with everything else scattered across the house. The life of a single mom is never easy, but when you are blessed with children like I have been, it's worth it. You make every day a blessing. I am so proud of you and how you have supported me through this and rooted me on. You are my biggest motivators and my biggest fans. I don't think any mom could be as lucky as I am to have you as my children. Thank you for being you. I also need to express my gratefulness for the family I was blessed to be born into and my parents, whose completely contrasting abilities and talents somehow made me who I am today. My mother for her creative wild spirit, her love of fine things, her expensive taste and her ability to live her life with class and dignity even in the toughest of times. My father, who always supported everything from my whims to my concrete plans and never tried to put me in a box of expectations—you have been so supportive that it wasn't until I was a grown adult with children of my own that I realized you thought all my ideas were amazing for the sole reason that you love me so much. I am so glad that failures lead to successes.

Last, thank you to my Party Style partners. I have loved working with you over the years—some of my greatest contributors, stylists, fans, friends, and confidants. Each of you that have contributed to the parties displayed on these pages have amazed me with your talent and originality. I appreciate each of you more than you'll ever know. Melissa Reyes, instantly a lifelong friend: our friendship is amazing. Your support and encouragement are never ending. We are like two schoolgirls who truly root for one another. Your cakes are out of this world, the centerpiece for any amazing soirée. Lauren of Capes & Crowns—we didn't know each other long before your belief in me started to inspire me. From the time we met, you always made me strive for bigger and better things—not only for myself but for the readers of *Party Style Magazine*. Thank you for supporting my brand from the beginning. I feel so grateful to have all of you and the fans of I Love Party Style supporting our little business every day. Words could never express the gratitude that I feel. I can only say thank you in the way I live my life and by giving back as much as I can, whenever I can—and by inspiring others to create a life they dream of, one step at a time. My mom used to say anything is possible, and she was right!

## ABOUT THE AUTHOR

Gemma Touchstone is the creative force behind the popular blog www.ILovePartyStyle.com, a leading industry blog and all-encompassing online party inspiration and idea-sharing community. Gemma is also the editor-in-chief of the publication *Party Style Magazine*. She is an accomplished designer, entrepreneur, and style maven. Gemma's Party Style brand reaches over 140,000 subscribers: 44,000 Facebook fans; 72,000 Twitter followers; and 35,000 Instagram fans.

Gemma resides in Newport Beach, California, with her daughter, Hannah, her son, Noah, and a sweet little terrier named London. Gemma started out as a floral designer for her company in 1999 and later transitioned into interior design. As others noticed her talent for all things creative, she was given amazing opportunities to design some of Hollywood's finest nurseries and playrooms. Gemma started blogging in 2013 and has gained readership and fans through her monthly newsletter, her weekly blog post, and party sharing. Gemma has styled countless celebrations for celebrity clients, everyday style seekers, and even her own friends' and family's parties, ranging from special events and theme parties to casual get-togethers. Gemma's style remains fresh, innovative, and inspiring to party-goers and party-throwers across the world. The near future plans for Gemma include writing new books (entertaining, party styling, and cookbooks) and designing a line of party goods to be sold nationwide. The next project for her is to tour the USA over the next year with the CAKE Expo, Sweets & Party Show. This consumer show is sure to bring all foodies and party people from near and far, and you can visit www.cake-expo.com for the details.